The Pie Place Café
COOKBOOK

Food & Stories Seasoned
by the North Shore

by Kathy Rice

Lake Superior
Port Cities Inc.

First Edition: June 2013

Lake Superior Port Cities Inc.
P.O. Box 16417
Duluth, Minnesota 55816-0417 USA
888-BIG LAKE (888-244-5253)

5 4 3 2 1

Library of Congress Cataloging-in-Publication Data

Rice, Kathy, 1951-
  The Pie Place Café cookbook : food & stories seasoned by the North Shore /
  Kathy Rice. – First edition.
      pages cm
  Includes index
  ISBN 978-1-938229-04-6
  1. Cooking, American – Midwestern style. 2. Dinners and dining – Minnesota – Grand Marais.
  3. Pie Place Café (Grand Marais, Minn.) 4. Pies. I. Title.
  TX715.2.M53R53 2013
  641.59776 – dc23   2013008210

Editors: Konnie LeMay, Ann Possis, Laura Zahn, Barb LeMasurier
Design: Tanya Bäck
Cover images: Katherine Goertz holding rhubarb by Mary Beams; *Hjördis* schooner in Grand Marais harbor by Paul Sundberg; Blackberry Peach Pie and Beef Stout Pie by Nadya Shkurdyuk; The Pie Place Café by Bob Berg.
Printer: Friesens, printed in Canada

In Loving Memory
This book is dedicated to Cheryl Polson.
She taught us about love, life and food.

Acknowledgements

WITH GRATITUDE

Writing a cookbook is a labor of love, one that requires many hours, many hands and many hearts.

We are grateful to all of you who have come to our table, savoring our food, sharing your lives with us, and loving us as much as we have come to love you. This cookbook is as much about each of you as it is about the food we serve. Food, and the love of family and friends, make coming to The Pie Place table an experience. It is why we do what we do.

Over the years, guests have asked us to write a cookbook featuring some of their favorite recipes. We hope that this humble attempt, sharing recipes and stories of lives that have touched ours, fills your life with as much joy and enchantment as it has ours.

I wish to express a special "thank you" to Larry Spaulding of the Print Shop in Grand Marais. Your expertise, co-creative spirit and friendship mean more than words can say.

My deepest gratitude also to Lake Superior Port Cities Inc. for taking on this project, and especially to my publishers, Paul and Cindy Hayden. As editor, Konnie LeMay took my hand and walked me through an uncharted forest (sometimes I swear I couldn't see the forest for the trees!), guiding me on how to bring these stories of my heart to life for others to read, enjoy and learn. I

Lake Superior, with its majesty and mystic presence that touches all who live beside it, is another North Woods neighbor and influence for whom Kathy is grateful. (photo by Nadya Shkurdyuk)

truly found a kindred spirit in Konnie, and she and all of the wonderful people at *Lake Superior Magazine* have been there for me at every bend. Their expertise, creativity and incredibly warm and friendly manner made my inaugural journey as an author rewarding beyond compare. They've helped me to make my dream come true.

I would like to express a special thank you to Nadya Shkurdyuk for assisting me with the food photography in this cookbook. With my passion for "vignetting" and your passion for photography, Nadya, we make quite a team. I couldn't be happier with the results.

I also wish to express a heartfelt thank you to Maryl Skinner. Your enthusiasm and encouragement throughout this creative journey has meant the world to me. Your presence in my life is a gift.

The stories on these pages were written over a number of years, almost part of a journal of remembrance for me. Because of that distance in time from beginning until now, several of the people on these pages have since passed on from this life. I still feel connected to them, and I am grateful for the gift of getting to know Joy Rousseau, Ed "Eddie" Anderson, Ed and Maud Joesting, Mildred "Millie" Johnson, Tom "Tommy" Eckel and Mike Morrison before they departed from us.

None of this would be possible, of course, without my restaurant family, and this book, as with all our endeavors, has been a collaborative effort. Each of us brings a lifetime of experience and expertise, creativity and passion to the creation and care of The Pie Place Café. The stories within these pages reflect the dedication of each person in our family to excellence and service. Though I have put pen to paper to write down these stories, it is truly the love and commitment of each person here that has made The Pie Place Café and this cookbook a reality. Our shared vision of group life, and the unlimited possibilities that it presents, have made all of this possible.

Finally, this cookbook would not have been written without the love, inspiration and guidance of our beloved family member, Cheryl Polson. She taught us about the nuances of cooking, created fabulous recipes and menus for us to prepare, and encouraged and nurtured us as we moved into new and often frightening territory.

Cheryl faced her extended illness and its challenges with profound strength, dignity and faith. She lived each moment of her life to the fullest, demonstrating a zest for living, and a love for her family that was expressed until her final breath. Though she has passed on, she is, and will continue to be, with us always.

Above all else, Cheryl taught us that a life worth living must be seasoned with love. In life, as with food … the first ingredient should always be love.

"We are grateful to all of you
who have come to our table."

Contents

THE FIRST INGREDIENT...

Food brings people together. Supper with family at the end of a hectic day, a weekend picnic with friends on a rocky shore snuggled around a blazing fire, an elegant meal to celebrate a person or an occasion, or dining at a favorite restaurant – the common thread is coming together in love, laughter and conversation.

Food evokes memories. Some are universal: Sunday dinner at Grandma's house with food that only she could make. Family traditions shared by a Christmas tree adorned with candy-colored lights. The rich aroma of roast turkey and stuffing that would make Pilgrims swoon with ecstasy. Some are specific to our North Woods: A walk in the woods gathering mushrooms to sizzle later in a cast-iron skillet. Sunburned shoulders and blackfly bites endured for the promise of a warm, flaky wild-blueberry pie. Pan fish pulled from a lake with a bamboo pole, then the smell of them swimming in butter alongside crispy, golden fried potatoes. A family around a hand-cranked ice-cream maker, eagerly awaiting cool, sweet ice cream topped with fresh-picked raspberries.

Yes, just the savory smell of certain foods can invoke remarkable memories and tug our heart strings.

The bringing together of food and people is what we've hoped to do since we first bought The Pie Place Café in Grand Marais, Minnesota, in 1995. I've described our menu as "fresh, regional food with a gourmet flair," but I also like the description written for *Lake Superior Magazine* by local writer Vicki Biggs-Anderson. She said our food was "like Grandma used to make ... presupposing Grandma was a cross between James Beard and Julia Child."

When I say "we," I truly mean that for The Pie Place. We are a close-knit group of friends and artists who consider ourselves family. Preparing and offering food is one aspect of our artistic endeavors. Making friends with customers and community members has become another treasured outcome of our café.

For years, we did Sunday dinner at The Pie Place, replete with old cut-glass dishes filled with sweet gherkins, olives, celery stalks and spiced crab apples (crudité of an earlier time). Cheryl Polson did the menu planning for the restaurant, and nobody did it better. True to the tradition of Sunday dinner, we served chicken and dumplings, pot roast, fried chicken and hearty stews during the cold winter months and picnic fare in summer, which, of course, meant barbecued chicken and ribs, potato salad, corn on the cob and pies made of seasonal fruit. Cheryl brought the memories of a collective family experience to The Pie Place, merging them to create her signature culinary style, "gourmet home cooking." In so doing, she touched the hearts of all who dined at our table.

I think I loved Sunday dinners at The Pie Place best, as there was a very special and intimate feeling about serving on that day. I went to each table and cleared the dishes in anticipation of that all-American dessert favorite ... pie! As I did, I saw something magical happen. People started talking of childhood memories. There was laughter and sometimes even tears, but good unabashed tears of remembrance at something rediscovered, dormant for so long.

One woman, her voice quivering, said, "I haven't had chocolate cream pie that tasted like this since my grandmother died. This is just like hers!"

One man, looking sheepish and a bit apprehensive, admitted, "I didn't clean my plate. Can I still have pie?"

The new location of The Pie Place Café is in downtown Grand Marais. (photo by Bob Berg)

"Absolutely," I replied. "Wow," he laughed, relieved and surprised at the fear of a childhood food taboo (no clean plate, no dessert). "Who knew that was in there?"

We create memories with food. We touch the hearts of those we love with food. Lifelong friendships and passionate love affairs flourish in the intimacy of a good meal shared. We nourish and help our children to grow healthy and strong with the flavorful goodness of food. We reach out, and bring solace to those in need with food. We heal with food, hearts as well as bodies.

For each recipe you'll find on these pages, we hold a memory of a friend or loved one who has touched us and forever – for us – flavored the food when we eat it. Some are tried, true and traditional recipes that you may recognize as old friends. We've included them here again because they represent favorites we serve or friends we celebrate.

Whether it's a hot dog on a stick roasting over a campfire or a five-course meal paired with fine wine, the most important thing we bring to each and every dining experience is love – love of food and love of people. The two are inextricably bound.

In our world, fast-paced and racing faster, the sharing of good food, lovingly prepared, anchors the heart and soul of who we really are. In spite of life's ups and downs, nothing has the power to bring us back to ourselves and what really matters quite like a home-cooked meal. No matter how simple the fare, when food is prepared with love, all is right in the world.

So please come to our table. Share with those you love the simple truth of food.

The world will be a better place because you do.

Breakfasts & Great Beginnings

EARLY MORNING BREAKFAST

Maureen Bazzett arrives in the early morning quiet when we prepare food for the day. A nurturing mother soul who strives for spiritual balance, her very presence calms the room. For me, light pours from her, love seeps through her skin. We can converse with words unspoken, heard by our hearts' ears.

The moment Maureen and Bob first walked into our restaurant, I felt a sort of spiritual love at first sight. When we spoke for the first time, I got a sense of "What took you so long to get here? You know this person, you love this person, even though you've just met five minutes ago." What a rare gift.

This morning, Maureen says, "I'm awake and Bob's still asleep, so I came for breakfast."

Maureen and Bob were raised in Michigan, another connection that we have. I am from there in my other life before the restaurant. They moved to Grand Marais to retire and enjoy life; I moved here to work and enjoy life.

Maureen and I share a compatibility, where we can talk and talk … or not. But always words seem to pour from our hearts – bridging, filling spaces, touching, awakening and bringing understanding … always, always coming together. Would that all people could have friends so comfortable and so dear.

"I'll have a scone, some coffee," Maureen says, "and an omelet. You know what I like."

"Listen to this song," I say, turning up the volume so Olivia Newton-John's "Grace and Gratitude" fills the tender quietude. Contemplative, we share the soul of coffee and song. A fellow traveler, morning paths crossing, touching and moving on until next time.

Maureen and Bob (way up at the top of the stairs) in a family portrait with their whole family. (photo by Teresa Belfanti)

Maureen talks of peace, non-violent ways of expressing and connecting one to all. She's risen above and beyond the box we were raised in, breaking out to learn about herself and God.

Bob and Maureen have created a living legacy in their children, the multicultural blend and harmony they endeavor to project to others. Maureen brings her beautiful children, and her grandchildren, to our poetry reading in the fall each year. They have become a part of us, threads in the fabric of who we are.

Bob and Maureen speak with great pride of family gatherings, where all come together in love. In this family diversity is the natural flow as is the flow of laughter like spring rain that regenerates its soil and brings new life.

An old Hebrew proverb asks: "The bird and the fish can fall in love, but where will they build their nest?"

I look at the family of this woman whom I've grown to love and answer, "Here. Right here."

Blueberry Lime Scones

The Pie Place is known for scones – warm, sugary and topped with clotted cream – a delightful way to start the day. As someone who loves our blueberry lime scones, Maureen is always happy to see them on our menu. People have asked about the names for our recipes. Some are simple acknowledgments of the most influential ingredients (like this one); some have a story behind them, as you will see later.

Serves 8

Amount — Ingredients

Amount	Ingredients
4 cups	all-purpose flour, divided, 3 cups plus 1 cup extra for handling the dough
3/4 cup	sugar, divided, 1/2 cup for recipe, plus 1/4 cup extra to sprinkle on top
4 teaspoons	baking powder
1/2 teaspoon	salt
1/2 pound	butter, very cold and cut into small pieces
1 medium	lime, the zest
1-1/3 cups	blueberries, frozen, medium sized, chopped
1/2 cup	half-and-half
1 large	egg

Instructions

Pulse 3 cups flour, 1/2 cup sugar, baking powder, salt and butter in a food processor (or mix by hand) until it is mixed to a grainy, pebbly state. Transfer to a medium-size bowl. Add the lime zest. Add the chopped frozen blueberries and toss these ingredients by hand to mix well.

Beat the egg into the half-and-half, then mix into the dry ingredients. Work quickly to form the dough, gently kneading it a few strokes. It may seem impossibly dry at first, but keep working with it, gently pressing it together. Eventually it will bind into a ball. If it resists coming together, you may add more half-and-half a few drops at a time. If the blueberries have thawed too quickly and the dough becomes sticky, toss in a handful of flour.

On a generously floured surface, form a disk about 8 inches across and 2 inches thick. Sprinkle the top liberally with sugar, using at least 1/4 cup, then with a large knife cut the disk into 8 wedges. At this point the wedges may be wrapped and stored in the freezer and baked as needed.

When you want to bake, place the wedges on parchment paper on baking trays. Lay the wedges out in a row, alternating tips facing in toward the center or out to the edge of the pan so as to have as much space between them as possible. You should put no more than six wedges to a flat baking tray, which will fit in most home ovens. The wedges tend to lean towards each other if they are too close together while they bake.

Bake for 18 minutes at 375° F in preheated oven, then check them and rotate the pan in the oven, bake an additional 5 to 12 minutes, depending on whether they were frozen solid when you began or were fresh from the prep table. They should be golden brown and firm to the touch when removed from the oven. Serve warm, with clotted cream.

On a Swing

When I see birches bend to left and right
across the lines of straighter, darker trees,
I like to think some boy's been swinging them ...

One could do worse than being a swinger of birches.
– from Birches by Robert Frost

Is there any joy quite like that seated with us on a swing?

Once we leave behind those carefree days of childhood, seldom do we again experience the delightful abandon of swinging.

The wooden seats, rough against your legs, and the thick-twisted rope beneath your small hands became your transportation into the realm of imagination and possibility. Our swing had a canopy of leaves overhead, and the warm summer sun would make lacy patterns on my arms.

After I got going, kicking my legs for all they were worth, I could almost touch those green leaves and the blue, blue sky beyond. I felt as if the ropes might let loose their hold – could let loose,

Kevin joins a friend in swinging with wild abandon. (photo by Kathy Rice)

should let loose – and fling me skyward like a tiny sparrow flitting through the clouds.

Sadly, as adults, we most often leave behind our swinging days. We enter instead an earthbound world of schedules, time frames and "have to dos," and the days fill themselves with little room for the free flight of a sparrow.

As restaurateurs, our days are crammed with preparing food, arranging flowers, going to the market for fish, selecting fresh produce and meats, putting fresh linens on the tables, lighting candles for the evening tables ... and the list goes on.

One particularly hectic day, I was hurrying to run yet another errand.

As I drove by the local childcare center, I spotted Kevin Kager, a customer and friend. He was on the swing set, joining the rhythmic back-and-forth fluttering with several children, looking for all the world like a giant on the small seat, his feet kicking high into the air, his head thrown back and long hair sweeping the earth with each pass.

A view from the beach looking toward the new home of The Pie Place Café and Harbor Inn. (photo by Nadya Shkurdyuk)

His smiling face radiated sheer joy – the joy of the moment, the joy of being in the company of children, the honest joy found on a swing.

I couldn't help but smile to myself.

I had to continue to make haste to finish my task, but in that moment, the tension and the should-do list of the day fell away.

Suddenly I remembered again my flight of the sparrow up into a canopy of green when all that mattered was how high I could swing. I felt, for a moment, that freedom on the seat of a swing.

Without ever seeing me, Kevin gave me a great gift – the gift of his swinging transformed my day.

"Is there any joy quite like that seated with us on a swing?"

Wild Rice Blueberry Waffles

I don't know about your family, but here at The Pie Place, we love breakfast for supper ... and as Kevin will attest, so do our guests. Wild rice and blueberries, both indigenous to northern Minnesota, add a delicately sweet yet earthy flavor and texture to these delightful waffles. Topped with warm blueberry compote, it's a meal that's sure to please.

Serves 6

Amount — Ingredients

Amount	Ingredients
2 cups	all-purpose flour
2 teaspoons	baking powder
1 teaspoon	salt
4	eggs, separated
1-1/3 cups	milk
1/2 cup	vegetable oil
1-1/2 cups	cooked wild rice

Blueberry Compote

Amount	Ingredients
2-1/2 cups	fresh blueberries, divided (or can use thawed from frozen)
1/3 cup	sugar
1/3 cup	water

Instructions

To prepare waffles: In a large mixing bowl, combine the flour, baking powder and salt. In a separate mixing bowl, beat egg yolks, milk and oil; stir into dry ingredients just until moistened. In another bowl, beat egg whites with an electric mixer until stiff peaks form; fold into batter. Fold in the wild rice with a spatula.

Bake in a preheated greased waffle iron according to manufacturer's directions until golden brown.

To prepare the Blueberry Compote: Combine 1-1/2 cups blueberries, the sugar and the water in a heavy small saucepan. Simmer 10 minutes until the berries burst. Add remaining 1 cup blueberries. Cook 6 to 8 minutes, stirring often. Serve warm. (Can be made two days ahead, refrigerated and gently heated in saucepan before serving.)

Waffles should be served hot and crispy. However, if you have several waffles to make, place them directly on a rack in a warm oven. You may garnish them with the warm blueberry compote or serve the sauce in a pretty bowl on the side so family and friends can help themselves. Don't forget your favorite maple syrup, we like our local Wild Country brand.

For variations, you could add half a cup of chopped pecans or tuck crisp smoked bacon between two waffles for a heartier breakfast or dinner.

"Wild rice and blueberries are
both indigenous to northern Minnesota and add a
delicately sweet, yet earthy flavor."

SISTER'S SPECIAL

When you own a restaurant – cooking and cleaning up all day, every day – it's great to get out, relax and have someone else do all of that. At least that's what we've found here.

In our small harbor town, all of us restaurant owners know each other, support each other and gladly frequent each others' establishments. No one seems to feel the need to be closed off and competitive. Here our fellow restaurateurs seem eager to lend a hand … or a bit of produce.

"I've got some extra fresh thyme. Come on over and help yourself!" or "Do you have any wild mushrooms? We're out" – as is the way in so many aspects within our small community, a helping hand gets extended.

While we enjoy getting to other local restaurants, we also love having other restaurant owners and chefs come here.

Betty Hamilton and her daughters Anna and Sarah used to own a local eatery called "My Sister's Place." Creative, hard-working women with huge hearts and a desire to see others succeed, they've become cherished Pie Place friends.

Sarah, Betty and Anna take a ride on the schooner Hjördis. (photo by Matt Brown)

Though busy in their own restaurant, they would still find time to come in for breakfast or call The Pie Place for carry-out or delivery. Anna and Betty both loved our sausage gravy, usually on biscuits, and they began to ask for it on other breakfast items like our hash-brown pie. Thus "The Sister's Special" became the catch word for their regular orders.

Suffice it to say that whenever our chef Josh saw two orders of "Sister's Special" written on a guest check, he knew who would get the breakfast. Though he prepares everything with attention, he'd take particular care with these special requests.

Betty, Anna and Sarah have always been there to lend a hand for us. When our ice machine broke during a blistering summer and we couldn't afford to fix it, Betty showed up with a replacement and refused to let us pay her. When I was the only server on some early days at the restaurant, Anna would come and help me to wait tables and to clean up. She even did dishes.

Their support has saved us and encouraged us. People like them make our village of Grand Marais an incredible place to live and work.

Pie Place Sausage Gravy

Our family took a trip to the Smoky Mountains many years ago, falling in love with that old Southern breakfast tradition of sausage gravy served over light, flaky homemade biscuits. After having it in several "Ma and Pa" restaurants, we replicated the recipe in a little cabin nestled beside a babbling stream. We sat at an old weathered table, having one of the best breakfasts of our trip and vowed if we ever owned a restaurant, we would be sure to "pass on the love!" It's become a critical part of those "Sister's Special" breakfasts and here is our version; it gets a "thumbs-up" from the Hamiltons.

Serves 4 to 6

Amount — Ingredients

Amount	Ingredients
1 pound	Jimmy Dean Original Sausage, we prefer this brand, but you can use others
4 Tablespoons	butter
1/4 cup	all-purpose flour
6 cups	half-and-half
	milk, to thin gravy as needed
	salt and black pepper, to taste

Instructions

Lightly brown sausage and break it up so that it is completely crumbled. Place the sausage in a strainer, draining the fat into a bowl for use in the gravy. Place the fat and butter in the skillet, melt and add flour. Stir for 2 minutes on medium-low heat. Using a flat whisk, stir in half-and-half and increase heat. Allow mixture to thicken until it reaches the bubbling stage to a gravy consistency. Add in the sausage. Season with salt and pepper to taste. Serve over warm, flaky biscuits.

We actually add 1 teaspoon of pepper to our gravy, as the traditional sausage gravy is rather peppery in taste. If you and your family prefer a less spicy gravy, reduce the pepper to accommodate your preference. If the gravy becomes too thick, it can be thinned with milk.

THE GALS OF NOVEMBER

November waves pound Artists' Point. (photo by Kathy Rice)

November arrives in Grand Marais, harkening the advent of another cold, blustery wind-tossed winter.

This is also the season of punishing gales, those infamous storms chronicled by singer/songwriter Gordon Lightfoot in his epic "The Wreck of the *Edmund Fitzgerald.*"

These storms are dangerous, despite the weather … and exhilarating. I remember well our first November in Grand Marais, when gale-force winds created a pounding surf that sent 10- to 12-foot waves crashing over the rocks and into the streets of our tiny village. Exciting (and more than a little scary), it gave us our first glimpse of the force of Lake Superior in all its power and fury.

Many visitors long to see that power. We have customers who plead, "Call us when the waves get big and we'll come up." So late fall can bring both waves and these hardy souls to our shores.

One cold November morning, four women bundled in warm woolen sweaters ambled in for breakfast. Hands wrapped around steaming mugs of coffee, their exuberance made them seem like a force of nature.

I asked where they were from and what had brought them to Grand Marais.

"We're the Gals of November!"

Confused, I asked them to explain.

They related that East Bay Suites, a newly renovated lodging on the site of the historic East Bay Hotel in downtown Grand Marais, had offered a getaway weekend called just that – "The Gals of November." To enter, participants were asked to write a short essay on why they needed a vacation.

The winner that year was a Wisconsin dairy farmer who hadn't had a vacation in 11 years. She wrote her essay while on her tractor. A hard one to beat! Rather than come alone, the farmer had gathered together her best friends to share in her Gals of November getaway. This was that group.

The November gales that weekend blew powerfully, crashing upon the rocky shore, but one Wisconsin Gal and her close friends found a happy harbor and a much-deserved weekend respite.

Strawberry Cream Cheese Stuffed French Toast

Even our Gals of November know on days of cold, blustery weather you need a warm and substantial start. This crisp French toast, stuffed with strawberry cream cheese and swaddled in warm maple syrup can make any day – even the chilly ones – start with a celebration.

Serves 4 to 6

Amount / Ingredients

Amount	Ingredients
1 loaf	French bread
2 packages (8-ounce size)	cream cheese, softened
1 cup	strawberry jam
2	eggs
1 cup	milk
1/8 teaspoon	cinnamon
	confectioners' sugar, for dusting

Instructions

Cut the French bread into 8 slices, about 1 inch thick. Then cut a pocket through the crust of each slice down about half to three quarters of the way, leaving the bottom 1/2 inch uncut. This makes a sort of fold open arrangement.

In a bowl, blend softened cream cheese and jam together until evenly combined. Open the slices and fill with the mixture, either spooning in or spreading on.

In another bowl, whisk eggs, milk and cinnamon until blended.

Heat the griddle or pan to medium-high heat. Dip stuffed French bread slices into the egg batter and grill on both sides until golden brown.

Dust each slice with confectioners' sugar and serve with warm maple syrup.

At the restaurant, we like to garnish each plate with a "fanned" fresh strawberry. Simply slice from the tip to green stem and fan. It creates a splendid presentation.

THE BLESSING TREE

Our family loves a beautiful fresh pine tree for Christmas. Sometimes we trek into the surrounding woods on our property, harvesting a tree together and often discover after dragging it home, "Hey, it didn't seem that big out there!" Other times we buy a fresh-cut tree from the local tree farmer. Either way, we love the pungent smell of the forest that assails our senses with the tree indoors.

Our tree is trimmed with handmade ornaments, birchbark strips, pine cones and tiny sparkling lights that look like fireflies amidst the boughs. The illuminated tree never fails to fill us with Christmas spirit.

We always have a tree in the restaurant, too. One year, our tree – "the best one yet" – stood awaiting the design concept for the season. Already adorned with lights that shone against its dark needles like tiny stars in a heavy winter sky, no inspiration arose for the decorations themselves.

Suddenly Cheryl Polson, surveying the sparkly branches, said, "Let's do a Blessing Tree. We can cut out white-paper snowflakes and have our customers write blessings on them to hang on the tree."

As with her menu planning, Cheryl had the gift of knowing how to nourish people's hearts.

Customers were so moved and excited by the idea of a Blessing Tree that they joined in as eagerly as children in art class. (I, however, apparently flunked snowflake cutting in elementary school!)

On Tuesday morning, our Pie Place regulars, who come for coffee and pastries after Mass, asked for paper. They cut out snowflakes and passed them around so each person could write their blessing.

Their enthusiasm was infectious. Soon everyone in the restaurant (even first-timers) was writing a blessing. Many made their way to hang them on the tree. Eyes sparkled, tired faces became animated and serious expressions dissolved into laughter and smiles.

Later in the week, three women came in for a bowl of hot soup after a rigorous day of snowshoeing. From Oregon, the retired art teachers proceeded to cut the most delicate and intricate snowflakes I'd ever seen – barring God's own crafting, of course!

I sadly let them know that I was snowflake-cutting deficient, so they gave me a lesson on the geometry of the art (geometry – no wonder I was having trouble). We talked and giggled, and I think dinner at The Pie Place may have been one of the highlights of their winter vacation.

After they left, atop the piles of paper scraps, I discovered a cache of snowflakes fit for a king.

Little things infuse our lives with inspiration and joy. At Christmas, or every day, reflecting on the blessings we give and receive will allow us to have kinder eyes through which to view the world.

Next time you walk in the snow, consider on the millions of flakes dancing through the air. Then in your mind, attach a silent blessing to one or two. The world will grow richer in the accumulating snows.

Gingerbread Scones

There's something comforting on a cold fall or winter morning about a kitchen perfumed with the smell of gingerbread, and these scones are reminiscent of old-fashioned gingerbread cookies

Makes 24

Amount | Ingredients

Amount	Ingredients
2-1/4 cups	all purpose flour
1 teaspoon	baking powder
1/4 teaspoon	baking soda
1 teaspoon	ground cinnamon
1/2 teaspoon	ground ginger
1/4 teaspoon	ground allspice
1/4 teaspoon	ground nutmeg
1/2 cup	butter, chilled
1/2 cup	currants
1/3 cup	molasses
3/4 cup	heavy cream

Lemon Butter

Amount	Ingredients
1/4 cup	butter, softened
1/4 cup	sifted powdered sugar
1 teaspoon	lemon zest
1 Tablespoon	lemon juice

Instructions

Preheat oven to 425° F.

In a large bowl combine the flour, baking powder, baking soda, cinnamon, ginger, allspice and nutmeg. Cut in butter with a pastry cutter until texture is crumbly. Stir in currants. Add molasses and heavy cream, stirring just until dry ingredients are moistened. Turn dough out onto a lightly floured surface, and knead 4 or 5 times.

On lightly floured surface, roll dough to 1/2-inch thick, cut with a 2-inch biscuit cutter and place on a lightly greased baking sheet.

Bake at 425° for 8 to 10 minutes, or until lightly browned.

Best served warm from the oven and topped with a flourish of lemon butter. Scones can be frozen after baking and pulled out for a quick morning treat.

For the lemon butter: Mix butter and sugar in a bowl until blended and then add zest and juice.

Recipe Notes

Recipe Notes

Soups &
Soul Warmers

A Three Sisters Gardener

Margaret inspects the season's harvest of corn.
(photo by Mary Beams)

Margaret Plummer-Steen lovingly tends the historic gardens at the Grand Portage National Monument. For nearly 20 years, she has planted, cultivated and harvested vegetables in the way of her Ojibwe ancestors.

Based on a 1791 seed inventory, Margaret selects varieties indigenous to those earlier times for the stockade gardens. She is the steward of heirloom seeds, a sacred task indeed.

Cultivating in our harsh northern climate requires patience, perseverance and hard work. Margaret is wise in the ways of gardening and has answered many questions over the years as we've strived to create a garden for The Pie Place.

Margaret once took us to a small village near the water's edge where birchbark lodges nestle among the pines, a part of the national monument. Near the village stood a cultivated plot called the "Three Sisters Garden." Planted in mounded earth, corn, squash and beans grew entwined, giving and receiving the nutrients they required to flourish.

These are well known among Native peoples as the Three Sisters. As Margaret explained, those early gardeners knew that what corn took from the soil was restored by the beans. Squash provided the shade that retained moisture in the soil. She added her own touch, sunflowers to feed the birds, thus keeping their hungry beaks from the other plants. This system created a delicate balance of give and take, the plants together strengthening the survival of all. I marveled at the wisdom of those early planters who understood the clear message of harmony and unity as a key to life.

Later, one crisp fall day, we loaded the car with a picnic basket, mulled cider and a camera, then headed off to take in the brilliance. At every bend in the road, we gasped at the foliage tinted red, bronze and gold. Quite by surprise, we arrived at the stockade. Margaret's old blue truck was in the parking lot. Though the monument was closed for the season, we hollered for Margaret and soon she appeared at the heavy lodgepole gate, a smile on her face. She opened the gate and let us into another world. A replica of the old kitchen – its stone hearth for cooking and root cellar and handmade wooden bowls and baskets to store grains – gave a glimpse of an earlier time. We felt the presence of the voyageurs, weary from paddling canoes laden with furs, who found refuge within these walls.

The gardens were just outside the kitchen. Margaret, her moccasins gently touching the earth, was harvesting beans, herbs and beautiful carrots in shades of orange, yellow and purple. We pulled them from the moist, fecund soil, knowing their entwined flavors would be the perfect addition to a savory fall stew.

Artichoke Bisque

Grilled vegetables create a rich, earthy flavor in this palate-pleasing soup. Great served year round, you'll love the texture of coarsely chopped vegetables and soft, velvety cream. Though you won't find artichokes in Margaret's garden, this is one of her favorite soups.

Serves 4

Amount / Ingredients

Amount	Ingredients
1	red bell pepper
2 cans (14-ounce size)	artichoke hearts, drained
	vegetable oil
1 Tablespoon	butter
1 small	onion, chopped
4 large cloves	garlic, finely chopped
1-1/2 cups	vegetable stock
1 cup	heavy cream
1 Tablespoon	cornstarch
1/2 cup	water
1/2 teaspoons	salt
Pinch	freshly ground black pepper
	Garnish with Cotija or Manchego cheeses, toasted pumpkin seeds or pine nuts.

Instructions

To prepare grilled vegetables, preheat a grill. Coat vegetables lightly with oil, place on grill, just away from the hottest spot. Turn occasionally with tongs to sear all surfaces. If you don't have a grill, or would prefer doing this step inside, use the broiler in your oven. Remove to a dish to let cool, reserving any juices that accumulate. Cut the vegetables and then small chop them in a food processor.

In a large saucepan, melt butter and sauté onion and garlic over medium heat, stirring constantly until onion is translucent. In saucepan with onion/garlic mixture, add vegetable stock, cream and grilled vegetables. Bring to simmer, stir to heat evenly.

In a small separate bowl, combine cornstarch and water. Slowly drizzle into saucepan while stirring to combine. The bisque will thicken slightly in 1 to 2 minutes to desired consistency. Add more cornstarch or water if necessary.

Add salt and a dash of pepper to taste. Serve with suggested garnishes, if desired.

GOAT TALES

For years Vicki Biggs-Anderson, then-editor of the *Cook County News Herald*, our newsworthy small-town paper, and her husband, Paul, came into the restaurant every night before the final pressrun to pore over layouts, cut sheets and eat a late-night supper. More friends than customers, we'd talk about the issues, laugh with them and enjoy their company.

Today Vicki calls herself a "recovering newspaper editor," and although a deadline no longer draws her every week, she still frequents The Pie Place. She now spends her days as gentlewoman farmer, tending a menagerie of goats, ducks, geese, chickens and dogs on a hobby farm near town.

Vicki writes a weekly blog, "Magnetic North," for our local radio station website. I always make time to read Vicki's column. She writes with heart and humor, and I find myself laughing or moved to tears and reading her words aloud to everyone near me.

As she recounts tales of her goats and other farmyard family, she is also chronicling life in our beloved North Woods community. Recently she wrote about life during and after her cancer diagnosis and treatment, about how Paul remained her rock of support and about those who share her life's journey.

Vicki and Paul take a leisurely stroll on their farm while the farmyard family peeks around the gate. The grounds of their farm are rustic and inviting, the perfect country retreat. (photos by Mary Beams).

Vicki is a "cancer transcender," as she most powerfully puts it. She has risen above her diagnosis and infused her column and the lives of others with hope, humor and honesty about meeting challenges head-on with courage.

Looking incredibly beautiful despite a loss of hair from the chemotherapy, she's been an inspiration. She's received emails, letters and calls from other women struggling with breast cancer and treatment; they have found a most incredible shoulder to lean on. While in the throes of treatment, Vicki learned about Qigong (chi-kung), an ancient Chinese healing art that uses meditation and movement to bring balance to the body's natural healing capabilities. She facilitates a weekly Qigong group in Grand Marais.

Vicki wrote about The Pie Place for *Lake Superior Magazine*. True to her form, the article had heart and humor, capturing the essence of who we are as a family and what our restaurant is all about.

Paul and Vicki are cherished Pie Place friends. Whenever they arrive, we can be assured of lively conversation, deep-belly laughter and the warm feeling of great companions.

Smoky Sweet Potato Soup

Lake Superior Magazine featured The Pie Place in its Restaurant & Lodging Guide several years ago in a story by Vicki. When asked to include one of our favorite soup recipes, there was no doubt which one to choose. A perfect fall soup, this one warms your tummy and gives you the chance to wrap your hands around a hot, steamy mug while savoring the (sometimes chilly) season.

Serves 12; makes 4 quarts

Amount	Ingredients
1 large	onion, chopped
1 cup	bacon, (about 5 to 6 slices) uncooked and chopped
1 cup	smoked sausage, (about 2 links) uncooked and cubed; andouille is great!
6 to 8	sweet potatoes, peeled and cut into 1/2-inch cubes
3 quarts	chicken stock
1 cup	heavy cream
	smoke flavoring to taste (we use liquid smoke)
1/2 teaspoon	dried oregano leaves
2	bay leaves, whole
	sour cream, for garnish

Instructions

Heat sauté pan. Add bacon, sausage and onion; sauté until onion is translucent and bacon is cooked; drain.

In soup kettle, add chicken stock, sautéed mixture, cubed sweet potatoes, smoke flavoring to taste and spices. Simmer until potatoes are tender (about 30 to 35 minutes). Remove bay leaves. Add heavy cream.

Cool the soup and purée in a food processor until coarsely textured (a quality retained from the sausage and bacon). Return to stove and heat gently until hot enough to serve.

Serve with a dollop of sour cream.

Our friendly chef Josh serves soup and smiles. (photo by Vicki Biggs-Anderson)

"Deep-belly laughter and the warm feeling of great companions."

Is There a Doctor in the House?

In the days when physicians still made house calls, medicine was practiced with little technology and lots of heart. The life of a country doctor was a hard one, with long, lonely hours, modest pay and late-night drives through swirling snowstorms.

Those were the days when doctors practiced medicine with what was on hand and often pulled miracles out of their black bags. To me, these country doctors were angels, creating healing out of almost nothing and saving their patients' lives.

Dr. Roger MacDonald was a country doctor in a remote North Woods community. He often didn't get paid for his services or got paid in chickens, eggs, garden produce or firewood.

He made do with what was available – one time he broke the front seat of his car to flatten it out for transporting a seriously

Roger, left, Jackie and their family enjoying their weekly Saturday lunch at The Pie Place. (photo by Mary Beams)

ill girl down to Duluth. There was no ambulance service. She stopped breathing on the way and he had to resuscitate her before continuing to the hospital.

Many years later, our beloved Dr. MacDonald wrote his memoirs, *A Country Doctor's Casebook*, *A Country Doctor's Chronicles* and *A Country Doctor's Journal*. They are written with eloquence and humility. They made me marvel at the tender tenacity of this remarkable man.

The books gave Roger an opportunity to see old patients, too. He told me about one book signing when a woman handed him an envelope with several hundred dollars inside. "You probably don't remember me," the woman explained. "When I was a much younger woman, you delivered all of my children. Each time I went into labor, we didn't have the money to pay you. Each time you told me, 'It's OK. Pay when you can.' You never made us feel ashamed that we couldn't pay."

"Well," she finished, "we can pay you now."

Every week, as regular as a yearly physical exam, Roger, his wife, Jackie, and the children come in for a relaxed Saturday lunch. A family of accomplished musicians and artists, their conversations are peppered with discussions of music, art, gardening, politics and writing.

Roger's practical nature comes through still; he never lets me bring a new dish for his dessert, but prefers the pie on the dinner plate. "I did dishes to help me get through medical school, and I know what a hard job that is," he says.

In these times of advanced and far-reaching medical technology, may the young physicians of today come to know that healing comes in many forms: compassion, empathy, love and the ultimate gift – the giving of oneself.

Boundary Waters Wild Rice Soup

Nothing says "home" like a pot of soup simmering on the stove, and we are a family who loves soup. When we were young (or sometimes older) the doctor would order rest and nurturing, healing soup. This recipe is one of the first soups we created for The Pie Place and it happens to be Dr. MacDonald's favorite. If he were still making house calls, I bet he might just prescribe this soup.

Serves 6

Amount	Ingredients
6 Tablespoons	butter
1 small	onion, chopped
1/4 cup	all-purpose flour
4 cups	chicken broth
1 cup	heavy cream
1/3 cup	sherry/white wine mixture
	(we use Piesporter, mixing 2 Tablespoons of sherry and 4 Tablespoons of wine)
1 cup	cooked wild rice
2 cups	mild cheddar cheese, shredded, we use Crystal Farms
	salt to taste
	white pepper to taste

Instructions

Melt butter in a medium soup pot, add onions and cook for five minutes until soft and slightly translucent.

Stir in flour with a whisk, stirring constantly, and cook for one minute. Add broth and whisk until smooth. Add cream and sherry/wine mixture, heating to simmer. Add wild rice, shredded cheddar, salt and white pepper to taste, and continue to stir and simmer gently for five minutes, until heated thoroughly and soup thickens slightly.

Wild rice is indigenous to the North Shore, and we love its earthy, nutty flavor. However, we tend to go easy with it in this recipe, as this is a rather delicate soup and it can be overpowered with too much rice. We start with 1/2 cup for a single batch, but let your taste buds be the judge. Same goes with the cheddar cheese. The Pie Place version isn't real cheesy, but if you like a bit more cheese flavor, go for it.

His Stitch in Time

Charlie takes a break from class at North House Folk School. (photo by Jeremy Chase)

Tall, his merry eyes peering over the rims of his spectacles – I imagine him suturing a wound with the same precision and attentiveness he employs as he weaves a basket of white, textured birch bark.

Dr. Mayo – "Charlie" to all who know and love him – is a constant and welcome presence at the North House Folk School and The Pie Place.

His medical profession actually brought him to his love of basket weaving.

Once when he was attending a Finnish Folk Art Festival, the Finnish woman at the event hired to teach birchbark basket weaving was lamenting that she was not allowed to teach without a physical here in the United States. Overhearing this, Dr. Mayo offered to assist.

"How many fingers am I holding up?" he queried, quite serious. "Can you stand on one foot? Say, 'Ah' and let me look at your throat."

In no time, she'd passed her physical and the class proceeded. When asked how she could repay him, Charlie replied, "May I take your class?" He was hooked.

That is very much Charlie. A mischievous elf, he weaves tales, as well as baskets, full of humor and wisdom. Born into a family of physicians – yes, that Mayo family – he completed his residency at the Mayo Clinic, then left to follow his heart into a practice of family medicine.

Retired now, you'll find Charlie teaching basket-weaving classes at North House, gathering birch bark in the forests along the Gunflint Trail or traveling to some remote part of Alaska to teach the time-honored craft of weaving vessels made of birch.

I've had the opportunity to take a basket-making class with Charlie and his fellow artisan, John Zasada. I've also gotten to know Charlie at the restaurant, where he often stops in for a bowl of soup and ends up in a conversation peppered with philosophical and thought-producing ingredients.

At Charlie's class, I met Elizabeth from Utah. We both were fascinated with our teacher and all he knew about birch and its timeless use in vessels among Native peoples of this country and of Scandinavia and Russia. Eager and pliable students, we came to love this gentle physician and maker of baskets as he skillfully wove his two lives together, one stitch at a time.

We most appreciated his can-do philosophy. "Anything that's worth doing," says Charlie, "is worth doing poorly. It's not about perfection but about what you're learning. It's just like life; it's all about the journey."

Charlie's journey has been particularly eventful and fruitful.

His healing hands have rewoven people's lives back together and his skillful hands have gently removed bark from a tree and created from it a vessel, beautiful and strong, before our eyes.

Mushroom Marsala Soup

Take time to sit with a friend, relax and savor a bowl of soup. This simple to prepare, yet elegant soup has a musky, complex flavor and pleasant texture. Like Charlie, it's sure to bring a smile to your face.

Serves 6

Amount — Ingredients

Amount	Ingredients
4 to 5 cartons (32 to 40 ounces)	white mushrooms, coarsely chopped
	butter, for sautéing
1 large can (49-ounce size)	chicken broth
1-1/2 cups	heavy cream
1/2 to 3/4 cup	Marsala wine
	salt and pepper, to taste

Instructions

Sauté mushrooms in butter. Put sautéed mushrooms in soup pot with chicken broth. Simmer gently until fully cooked, about 45 minutes. Purée in food processor or with an immersion hand blender until smooth, but still textured. Add heavy cream and Marsala. Add salt and pepper to taste.

Using a variety of mushrooms, including dried, can change the texture and blend of flavors.

TELLER OF TALES, SINGER OF SONGS

He gathers musical notes, one by one, like wildflowers in a field. His lyrics, the raindrops that wash the petals clean, spill out emotions that run in silvery sheets to cleanse the heart.

Jon Vezner is a teller of tales and singer of songs.

We met Jon a few years ago when hunger led him to our door. We came to know him by pie slice and song – two passions he merged subtle and sweet in the café. Tall and lean ,with a felt beret perched on his long curly hair, he'd sit at a table and sing – yes, sing – the praises of his blueberry pie.

Jon always brings an entourage of creative and musical friends from around the world. A Minnesotan by birth, he lives now in Nashville and he founded the annual Unplugged Concert at the North House Folk School as a way to say "thank you" to the community. The concert benefits the Educational Endowment Fund for North House.

Comfortable and quirky, Jon fits like a local when he comes here. One would hardly realize that he holds a Grammy award for his work and hobnobs with other famous folk back in Nashville. So involved in making certain all goes well with the Unplugged Concert and its performers arriving from around the world, Jon has been known to wander off without warning during our conversations. But I take no offense; Jon is one of the most sensitive and talented people I know.

Once Jon brought me a CD of new music and asked me to listen and guess which songs he had written. The next day when he came back, I correctly picked out every one.

"How did you know?" he marveled.

"You have a huge heart," I told him, "and these songs were written by someone with a tender heart."

This minstrel and his musician friends touched us with their songs. In return, we've fed them, shared our home with them and invited them into our hearts.

All of us hide away inside us treasure boxes – chests of memories and long ago images, taken out on rare occasion, but always there for us just the same. Sometimes when we least expect it, a song flings that lid wide open and out come emotions.

Music connects us in a visceral way; songs are our shared communion. Musicians reveal themselves through a song, and in the revelation, you find you are revealed as well.

Jon has strummed his way into the hearts of those who live in our village of Grand Marais. It's a friendly place, easygoing and unpretentious. It's a place where you are appreciated for who you are, not who you know. It's one more thing we love about this place that we call home.

And, I think, it's what Jon, the witty singer of pie praises, loves about it, too.

I'm gonna go where my spirit sings.
I don't care if it's by wheels or wings.
I'm gonna follow what I feel,
That leads me to the real thing.
– Jon Vezner, "The Real Thing" about Grand Marais

Jon brings music to our shores every year.
(photo courtesy Jon Vezner)

Curried Acorn Squash & Apple Soup

The leaves are changing to brilliant red, yellow and orange, the air is crisp and filled with the earthy fragrance of fall, and the bounty of the harvest is ready to fill your table with goodness. Our friend Jon comes to the North Shore every year in the fall, and every year we make him a pot of his favorite spicy squash soup. Once you try this soup, you might want to sing about it, too.

Serves 12

Amount — Ingredients

Amount	Ingredients
2 medium	acorn squash (about 3 pounds), halved
1/4 cup	butter
4-3/4 cups	chicken broth, divided
4	Granny Smith apples, peeled, cored and cut into small pieces
2	baking potatoes, peeled and coarsely diced
1-1/2 Tablespoons	curry powder
3/4 teaspoon	ground red pepper
1/2 teaspoon	ground cinnamon
1 teaspoon	salt
2 cups	heavy cream
2 Tablespoons	honey

Instructions

Preheat oven to 350° F.

Place squash halves, with seeds removed, cut side down, on an aluminum foil-lined baking sheet. Bake at 350° for 45 minutes, or until tender. Scoop out pulp, discarding shells; set baked squash aside.

Melt butter in a soup pot over medium heat; add 4 cups chicken broth, apples, potatoes, curry powder, ground red pepper, ground cinnamon and salt. Cook over medium heat, stirring often, 25 to 30 minutes or until apples and potatoes are tender. Remove from heat, and cool for 5 to 10 minutes.

Process squash pulp, broth mixture and remaining 3/4 cup chicken broth, in batches, in a food processor or blender until smooth, stopping to scrape down sides.

Return puree to the pot. Stir in heavy cream and honey, and simmer, stirring occasionally, 15 to 20 minutes or until thoroughly heated. Be careful not to boil the soup once the heavy cream has been added. Serve immediately and enjoy.

JOY

Joy in images from her girlhood in Grand Portage. (photos from the Duhaime family)

The very appearance of certain people in a room brings sunshine and joy to those around them.

These people tap a deep, overflowing well of compassion within them. They never look at what they need, but rather how they can meet the needs of others.

We've known Joy Rousseau for many years.

An "Indian Lady," as she calls herself, her exuberant warm and giving ways and her ready smile have endeared her to us over the years – first as a Pie Place guest and now as our friend.

Small in stature but with a heart as huge as the sun, Joy is the one who plans cheerful birthday parties with gifts and love for the elders.

Joy is the one who gives fresh-baked cookies and warm hugs to the children.

Joy is the one who makes sure that no one who is sick or in need is alone.

When Joy comes into the restaurant, she often brings friends who need a steamy bowl of soup, which we can provide, and then she warms away their loneliness with her attention and conversation.

Joy loves to stop "for a visit," as she says, and for a bowl of soup. But she declines one of our favorites:

"No wild rice," she adds with a mischievous gleam. "I ate too much of that when I was a girl!"

We serve it up and for just a short while, Joy sits still and sips her soup. Then, like a whirlwind of snow rising to the sky, she's off again looking for another place to bring her gifts.

Joy – I have never met a more perfectly named soul.

K'weedjeewin
Tibishko mong punae cheega/eehn.

I am by your side
Like a loon, always nearby
– from Ojibway Ceremonies by Basil Johnston

Baked Potato Soup

One of the first soups we created during the early days of The Pie Place, this soon became a favorite of our guests like Joy, who enjoyed a warming bowl. If you enjoy the earthy, roasted flavor of a baked potato, you'll love this soup. Don't forget the garnish … after all, it's what we adore about a great baked potato.

Servings: 6

Amount	Ingredients
8 to 10	Idaho potatoes, baked and peeled while hot
2 to 4 cups	milk
1 large can (49-ounce size)	chicken broth
1/2 pint	half-and-half (8 ounces)
1/8 to 1/4 cup	white wine, we like Piesporter
	garlic salt, to taste
	white pepper, to taste
1 Tablespoon	heavy cream
	garnish with sour cream, cooked and crumbled bacon, shredded cheddar cheese, sliced green onions

Instructions

Bake the potatoes until soft and then peel them while they are still hot. Blend them in a food processor with milk (or use hand-held electric whip) until smooth. Transfer to a pot and add chicken broth, half-and-half, wine, garlic salt, white pepper and heavy cream.

Garnish with sour cream, crumbled bacon, shredded cheese, and green onions.

FLY THE FRIENDLY SKIES

Maggie McMahon made a career of "flying the friendly skies." Though retired now, she spent years as a flight attendant, traveling between the United States and the Orient. She's traveled extensively in Japan and exudes an energy that's worldly, yet grounded and engaging.

Maggie and her husband, Tom, own a cabin on the shore of Lake Superior. It provides a quiet, peaceful respite from the hectic life of frequent air travel and a family business.

We first met Maggie at Northern Impulses, the art gallery and gift shop we owned during our early days in Grand Marais. She became an avid collector of Mary Lear's pastel landscapes, procuring several original pieces to adorn the walls of their cabin. Mary is one of our Pie Place family.

Maggie, playfully called "Magpie" by our waiter Jeremy, drives a snappy silver Audi A4. It's this world traveler's means of "flying" to the North Shore for solitude and regeneration.

Two of our Pie Place clan, Josh and Jeremy, have gazed with longing at her racy little car.

"Take her for a spin," Maggie has generously offered more than once. "She'll give you quite a ride!"

On several occasions, she's been pulled over – "The car just looks like it's going fast!" she insists. I think it's just a good excuse for the officers to check out her car.

Maggie loves our Salsa Corn Chowder, sassy with more than a little spice. Somehow this does not surprise me. And it never fails that Maggie will arrive at The Pie Place every time her favorite soup is on the menu.

"Maggie will be here any day," I declare. "Let's make extra chowder."

Soon she arrives, a dazzling smile on her face, eager to see us and dine with us. She rarely leaves without a half gallon of her favorite chowder and a fresh loaf of bread.

We love Maggie and Tom. They bring the far world with them and there's so much to talk about when they arrive. Their friendly, caring manner makes them feel like family … which, of course, they are.

Salsa Corn Chowder

The piquant, palate-pleasing flavor of this chowder keeps Maggie flying to the North Shore. We serve it each year at North House Folk School's "Chowder Experience," and people just can't seem to get enough. If you like food with a bit of a kick, you'll want to spice up your menu with this awesome chowder.

Serves 6

Amount — Ingredients

Amount	Ingredients
1-1/2 cups	chopped onion
2 Tablespoons	butter
1 Tablespoon	flour
1 Tablespoon	chili powder
1 teaspoon	ground cumin
1 package (16-ounce size)	frozen corn
2 cups	salsa (we use Pace medium salsa)
1 can (14-ounce size)	chicken broth
1 jar (4-ounce size)	chopped pimientos, drained
1 package (8-ounce size)	cream cheese, room temperature
1 cup	milk

Instructions

Sauté onions in butter in large saucepan. Stir in flour, chili powder and cumin.

Add corn, salsa, broth and pimientos. Bring to a boil; remove from heat. Gradually add 1/4 cup hot mixture to cream cheese in a small bowl, stirring until well blended. Add cream cheese mixture and milk to saucepan, stirring again until well blended. Cook until heated thoroughly. Do not boil.

"Maggie will be here any day," I declare.
"Let's make extra chowder."

CELEBREMOS

Celebremos
todo aquello que nos connecta
uno al otro

Let us Celebrate
All that Connects
Us to One Another

As restaurateurs, we relish as rare treats those infrequent instances of dining out. It's sheer bliss – one might say heaven – to relax, savor the flavors and be waited on.

Chefs love to share recipes and tales of the kitchen. We love to cook for

Maria and Tomas Silva on one of their visits. (photo by Mary Beams)

other chefs, knowing how much we enjoy the experience and wanting to give them the same.

One warm summer day, a party of four guests came to The Pie Place for lunch. Only after they had eaten, enjoying the food and exclaiming about the "different layers of flavor," did we discover that they owned a Mexican restaurant in the Twin Cities.

They use cherished family recipes, passed down from their mothers in Mexico.

We connected deeply with our guests, as people do when swapping stories of family and food. Later that day, as our new friends were leaving Grand Marais, they stopped by the restaurant to drop off several brightly colored containers and the promise that they would visit us when they returned.

After they left, we opened the containers. Out wafted the earthy smell of stone-ground corn tortillas, spicy chilies and cilantro and guacamole – a feast laid out before us, their marvelous way of saying, "Thank you."

Sampling the food, we thought of grandmothers, we imagined gnarled hands patting out corn tortillas on a sun-warmed stone, red chilies hanging clustered from a hook on an adobe wall and an earthen pot of cilantro growing on a sunny window ledge. We saw a heavy oak table laden with colorful pottery dishes, awaiting the succulence of this meal.

Suddenly, we were back in our own kitchen, and about to prepare the dishes to serve to our guests that evening.

But for a few brief moments, we dined in Mexico, connected to a culture and celebrating the Silva family, our new friends.

Turkey Chipotle Chili with Chocolate

While hard pressed to duplicate the robust and authentic flavors in Maria & Tomas' "kitchen picnic" for us, we chose this recipe as a worthy gift for them and for you. You'll love the subtle hint of chocolate; it's the perfect end note for this extremely spicy chili.

Serves 8

Amount — Ingredients

Amount	Ingredients
1 Tablespoon	vegetable oil
2 cups	diced onion
1 cup	chopped red bell pepper
1 teaspoon	minced garlic
1-3/4 pounds	ground turkey breast
3 Tablespoons	dark brown sugar
2 Tablespoons	Ancho chili powder, this has a kick, some may prefer regular chili powder
1 Tablespoon	unsweetened cocoa
1 teaspoon	ground cumin
1/2 teaspoon	freshly ground black pepper
1/4 teaspoon	salt
2 cans (15-ounce size)	pinto beans, rinsed and drained
2 cans (14.5-ounce size)	diced tomatoes, not drained
1 can (14-ounce size)	chicken broth
2	chipotle chiles, from those canned in adobo sauce, minced
2 ounces	unsweetened chocolate, chopped
	garnish: green onions, chopped, and sour cream
	lime wedges, optional

Instructions

Coat soup pot with vegetable oil and heat on medium-high setting.

Add diced onion, red bell pepper, garlic and turkey. Sauté 8 minutes or until turkey is lightly browned and vegetables are tender. Add remaining ingredients except for chocolate. Stir until blended and bring to a boil. Reduce heat and simmer 15 minutes or until slightly thick, stirring constantly. Add chopped chocolate, stirring until melted.

Garnish with sour cream and green onions. Some folks like to squeeze a bit of lime juice into the soup.

For those who find this too spicy or don't like lots of kick, try 1 or no chipotle chile.

A Good Man

Russell is a good man and, in fact, his name is Russell Good.

Though he no longer resides in Grand Marais, having left to be near his elderly parents and young grandchildren (including one Johnny B. Good!), Russ remains a cherished Pie Place friend. How could he not be; he was there for us in so many ways in those early "growing pains" of The Pie Place.

Russ dined with us, believed in us, supported us and loved us as only a truly good friend would do. His warmth and caring infused us with hope, his good-natured teasing and humor made us laugh and lightened a heavy load. He brought light to our life and frequently stood in the gap as we made our way, step by step, to the restaurant that we are today.

One cold winter day, up to our ears in mashed potatoes, dirty dishes and many feet of snow to shovel, our water heater in the restaurant breathed its last breath.

Hearing of our dilemma, Russell brought us an early Christmas present.

We offered to pay him off as we could, but he shook his head, an empathetic look in his eyes. "When I was down and out, with two little boys to take care of by myself and no money for food, someone extended a helping hand. Now it's you who need it, and it's me who's extending a hand to help. Someday you'll do the same for someone else."

After he left, we found a card on the kitchen counter. Opening it, we read, "Do not withhold good from those to whom it is due when it is in the power of your hand to do so." Proverbs 3:27

Russell used to tease us about how good our homemade "Campbell's Soup" was. One year for Christmas we filled a huge stocking with cans of Campbell's Soup and presented it to him. He laughed all the way to his shiny red truck.

The greatest gift Russ gave us, though, was his friendship. He believed in us when few others did and from a place deep in his heart, he saw our vision and supported it without hesitation, asking nothing in return.

That's the kind of man our friend Russell is ... a good man!

Russell holds the results of his good catch. (photo by Michael Good)

Beef & Barley Soup

"Mmmmm, good …" Despite the relentless teasing about store-bought soups from Russ, our soups at The Pie Place are homemade and this savory one is no exception. Try this grown-up version that the whole family will love.

Serves 6 to 8

Amount — Ingredients

Amount	Ingredients
2 teaspoons	vegetable oil
1-1/2 pounds	eye-of-round steak, cut into 1/2-inch cubes
1/4 teaspoon	freshly ground black pepper
1/4 teaspoon	salt
1-1/2 cups	onion, sliced
2 cups	carrots, sliced 1/2 inch thick
2 packages (8-ounce size)	fresh white mushrooms, sliced
1/2 cup	red bell pepper, chopped
2 cloves	garlic, minced
6 cups	beef broth
1/2 cup	uncooked pearl barley
2 Tablespoons	fresh basil, chopped
1/4 teaspoon	crushed red pepper
1 can (14.5-ounce size)	diced tomatoes, not drained
1 sprig	fresh thyme

Instructions

Heat vegetable oil in a large nonstick skillet over medium-high heat. Sprinkle beef evenly on all sides with salt and black pepper. Add beef and onion to pan, sauté 5 minutes, turning to brown the meat on all sides. Remove beef mixture from pan, place in an electric slow cooker.

Add carrot and mushrooms to pan, sauté 5 minutes. Add bell pepper and garlic; sauté 2 minutes, being careful not to scorch or burn the garlic. Add carrot mixture, broth, and remaining ingredients to slow cooker, stir well. Cover and cook on high, 1 hour. Reduce heat to low, cook 6 hours. If necessary, skim off fat from the meat or foam from the barley during the cooking process. Discard thyme before serving.

If you don't have a slow cooker, a soup pot will work just fine. Simmer the soup for approximately 2-1/2 hours, until the meat is tender and the barley is soft.

ONE MORE STORY

Sometimes you can feel it, deep down inside of you. That moment when you know that something isn't quite finished, when another story is waiting to be told.

It's not unlike cooking really. Something inside of you says, "It's done" or sometimes it says, "Something more needs to be added."

David and Mary Jane Nelson, bright, creative and energetic people, have brought their stories to our table for many years.

David's fish stories make us laugh and his ice luminaries, which look like fine crystal, have graced our porch with shimmering candlelight in winter.

Mary Jane is savvy and in the know about politics, and, like me, is an avid reader.

We've swapped titles of our favorite books and created our own instant mini book clubs, the two of us in animated discussion of a story's merit and meaning.

David and Mary Jane love the life they've created on the North Shore and savor the experience of sharing it with those they love.

Often Mary Jane will call and ask us to cater a dinner party for visiting friends, thus freeing her to be with them completely. She and David love our Beef Bourguignonne (the French spelling!) and warm, crusty loaves of fresh baked French bread, a perfect companion for dinner in front of a crackling fire.

They call frequently to request roasted vegetable soup, custom made just for them, featuring organic vegetables of their choice from our local food co-op.

We love nothing better than to provide someone with their heart's desire, and David and Mary Jane are generous in expressing their gratitude when we do.

David and Mary Jane on the rocky shores of Lake Superior. (photo courtesy David and Mary Jane)

One day, as Mary Jane and I were talking books, I asked her what or who had made her so passionate about reading.

"Oh, my father," she said, eyes shining. "He loved to read. There were four children in our family, and he wanted all of us to love reading as much as he did. I remember him saying, 'This is an awfully good book. Why don't you read it, and then we can talk about it.' He really wanted to share the stories he read. As children we learned about giving and receiving in this way. Our family reading was a reflection of a real give and take."

"As soon as we were old enough, we enjoyed reading the same book and discussing it in the evening around the dinner table. Dad would read the first 30 or 40 pages, tear them out of the book and pass it to my sisters. When one had finished, they would pass it on to me, and so on. This continued until we had all finished the chosen book, at which time my father would re-assemble it and tie it securely with twine, ribbon or whatever happened to be available."

Many book lovers might be appalled by this practice, but I was deeply moved by Mary Jane's story.

What a wonderful way to teach one's children about so many things they would need in life… sharing, opening their minds to learning, formulating thoughts and feelings and expressing them, and the importance of those simple, yet profound moments in life.

As I imagined these precious stories read and shared, page by torn page, then discussed in animated voices around a dinner table, I felt drawn to see these treasured volumes, bound with string. I asked Mary Jane if she had any of those books.

When her father passed away, she explained, she and her family were inheritors of the family's "bound books."

At our next luncheon "book club," Mary Jane brought in a picture of her treasured books. I could almost smell the aged leather covers, worn smooth by young hands, and the torn yellowed pages bound tenderly within; the smell of a story well-written. In my mind's eye, I watch the father gently tearing pages out of a beloved book and passing them to his child, her young mind eager for the story to begin.

Our parents give us so many gifts – some last but a moment, others endure a lifetime.

Sometimes a story is not just a story. What lies behind it tells a tale as well; that's one more ingredient added to a rich and savory stew so that you can just feel it when it's done.

"It's not unlike cooking, really;
Something inside of you says, 'It's done'
or it says, 'Something more needs to be added.'"

Chicken & Roasted Vegetable Soup

This hearty soup is healthy, flavorful and perfect for cool summer or late fall nights. Mary Jane and David love broccoli and carrots, but you can use your favorite veggies. We are members of a local CSA (Community Supported Agriculture) group. If you are lucky enough to get fresh vegetables from your CSA, farmer's market or garden, go ahead and experiment. The soup's flavor will vary according to what you choose, but that is part of the fun. We love garlic, but that ingredient also can be adjusted to your taste preference.

Serves 4 to 6

Amount — Ingredients

Amount	Ingredients
1	whole chicken
3 to 6 cloves	garlic, peeled
2 cans (49-ounce size)	chicken broth
4 to 6 Tablespoons	olive oil
1 head	broccoli, cut into florets
1 bunch	carrots, cut on the diagonal in 1/4-inch slices
8 to 10 stems	fresh thyme leaves

Instructions

Preheat oven to 400° F. Rinse chicken in cool water. Place whole chicken in stock pot with chicken broth, garlic and fresh thyme leaves. Bring to a boil, reduce heat to medium-low heat and simmer for approximately one hour, until chicken is fully cooked. Remove chicken from stock and set aside to cool. Remove thyme stems. When cool enough to handle, remove chicken from bones and discard carcass.

While chicken is cooking, toss vegetables in olive oil, place on baking sheet, and roast in oven for 30 to 45 minutes, stirring occasionally. Vegetables should be roasted to golden brown and tender when poked with a fork. Add roasted vegetables and chicken pieces to stock and season with salt and pepper to taste.

*"The soup's flavor will vary
according to what you choose,
but that is part of the fun."*

Recipe Notes

Recipe Notes

Salads, Sauces, Sides & Celebrations

Jean's Greens

When not tending gardens, Jean and her husband, Harold, enjoy getting out to visit local wonders like Pigeon River. (photo courtesy the Husbys)

I can imagine her, even now.

It's early morning as she bends over dew-kissed patches of tender greens, a floppy straw hat on her head. She gathers a veritable collage of lettuce, herbs and tiny yellow, orange and blue flowers.

Placing them in a basket, she carries them to the sink, her hands caressing each leaf and every flower, readying them for their great debut.

Like gardener Jean Husby's day, our day also begins early. We roll dough for freshly baked pies, simmer soups in large pots on the stove and whisk together the ingredients that will become sauces and dressings. Ours is a palette of flavors, merged to awaken, nourish and delight the senses.

She comes bearing gifts, offerings laid on the altar of this day. Her greens and edible flowers will be used to create works of culinary art – the salads for our Pie Place customers.

We feel the reverence and care with which Jean has gathered and prepared her garden bounty. We pay it homage by taking care in what we prepare from it.

The plate is our canvas, awaiting a serving of culinary artwork for our hungry guests. Jean brings her gifts to us, and we share them in the brush strokes of a new day.

Black Bear Blueberry Salad

Jean used to bring us beautiful organic greens every morning, and since fresh greens are what make this salad so memorable, it's no surprise that Jean loves it. This summer favorite is served on a bed of organic greens with roasted chicken, a smattering of plump blueberries and drizzled with our sweet, creamy orange dressing. It brings out summer – no matter the time of year.

Serves 4; dressing makes 4 to 6 servings

Amount   Ingredients

Amount	Ingredients
12 cups	mixed organic baby greens
2 cups	shredded roasted chicken
1/2 cup	toasted slivered almonds
1/4 cup	diced green onions
1/2 cup	diced celery
4 ounces	Gouda cheese, sliced into sticks of 1/4-inch by 1-1/2 inch
1-1/3 cups	Mandarin oranges (or 8-ounce can, drained)
1 cup	blueberries, fresh or thawed frozen

Creamy Orange Dressing

1 cup	mayonnaise
1/2 cup	sour cream
1	orange, for zest and juice
1/4 cup	orange juice concentrate
4 to 6 Tablespoons	honey, to taste

Instructions

Divide mixed greens evenly among four large plates. Add ingredients to build your salad in the following order, dividing evenly: shredded chicken, diced green onions, celery, Gouda cheese batons, Mandarin oranges, blueberries and toasted almonds.

To prepare creamy orange dressing: In a bowl, combine the ingredients and blend with a wire whisk until smooth. Cover and chill for a few hours. Drizzle salad with the dressing to desired personal taste and serve.

CISCO FOR THE WHITE HOUSE

The life of a commercial fisherman was and is a hard one. But Lake Superior proves a powerful lure for those men whose blood runs for the solitary waters, the feel of the cold wet net in their calloused hands and the smell of fish in their nostrils.

These fishermen with sun-weathered faces search the sometimes ominous, always remarkable freshwater seascape, chugging to and from their nets in their equally weather-worn boats. After a morning's catch gets hauled on board, an entourage of shrieking gulls trails the boats to shore, anticipating a delectable breakfast of fish heads and innards tossed into the Lake at the dock.

Lill Anderson was a fisherman's wife. Irish and full of laughter and life, she baked pies for her husband and six small children. Her pies, greatly savored at her home, soon became a way to earn a little extra income to help feed and clothe her hungry and rapidly growing family. It filled her with pleasure to know that those in the little fishing village of Grand Marais were as delighted by the fruits of her labor as were her family.

We've laughed a boatload – Lill, her daughter, her niece and I – big, deep-belly laughs that make you feel healthier from the very act. Lill claims it's the passion of the Irish in her, and I believe this is true.

Lill told me that her husband, Ed, once was commissioned to provide fish at a White House dinner for Franklin D. Roosevelt. Ed accepted the honorable task with the humble demeanor of the hard-working Swede that he was. He set about netting several pounds of Lake Superior cisco to grace the president's table.

Ed Anderson at work on the water and smoking fish at his fish house in winter. (top photo by M.J. Humphrey; facing photo courtesy Anderson family)

From his old fish house on the shore of Grand Marais harbor, he unloaded his catch, smoked the fish and packed them on ice for the boat and train trip to Washington, D.C. It was a proud moment.

In the years since, the beloved fish house burned to the ground and Ed, a hard working fisherman to the end, has passed away.

And Lill still bakes pies, now for her grandchildren. And she still dresses up to go out to shop for groceries.

One day, while in for lunch, Lill showed me a card she'd just picked up at Joynes Ben Franklin, our modern-day version of an old general store.

"Every year on our anniversary, I get Ed a card and lay it on the piano," she told me, her eyes misty and far away.

She showed me her wedding ring. "He's still my husband, and strange as it may seem, I'm still married. I love him as much today as I did back then. He fed a president, but more important than that, he was a good husband, father and fisherman. I think that's what he would want us to remember."

Though commercial fishermen still make their living from our Great Lake, it's a profession much reduced in numbers and a far cry from the early days, when the pundits of the East would look to a Grand Marais fisherman to be the purveyor of cisco for a newly elected president.

Smoked Salmon & Caper Pasta Salad

Some of us have fed presidents, but most of us are honored to prepare meals for our family and friends. Everyone is important when it comes to good food. This pasta salad is a great summertime dish featuring smoky salmon and peppery capers. We smoke our own salmon, but any good fish market can provide you with what you need. (Our smoker isn't like the one that Ed used, but I like to believe he'd approve heartily of our humble attempt.) If smoked fish is not available, poached salmon would be a tasty substitute. Tossed in a creamy dressing, it is fit for a president …and your family, too.

Serves 4

Amount   Ingredients

Amount	Ingredients
6 to 8 ounces	smoked salmon, boned and lightly flaked
1/2 jar (3.5-ounce size)	capers, drained
1 pound	uncooked pasta, your choice, we like penne

Easy Dressing

1 cup	mayonnaise, we always use Hellmann's
1/2	fresh lemon, squeezed
2 Tablespoons	fresh dill, chopped
	half-and-half (to thin dressing)
	salt and pepper, to taste

Instructions

Cook pasta to your desired doneness (we find firm, or al dente, is nice for pasta salad) and per package instructions. Rinse cooked pasta in cold water to stop the cooking and keep it firm.

Flake salmon, drain capers and add to pasta.

Mix mayo, dill and lemon for dressing, then thin with half-and-half to desired consistency. If pasta remains dry, add a bit more mayonnaise and half-and-half. Salt and pepper to taste.

WE ARE THE WORLD

It has been said that it takes a village to raise a child. Sometimes it just takes a family with a whole lot of love and a global vision of the world and its people.

Our customers, Don and Betchen Oberdorfer, their daughter, Erin and her beautiful little girls have charmed their way into our hearts. Don and Betchen lived for many years in India, Don having grown up there with his parents.

The couple ultimately returned to India, where Don served as a minister.

Don and Betchen are people whose hearts are full of love, and it came as no surprise when their daughter adopted McKayla, who is Native American, and Savita from India. Shortly thereafter, Erin had a baby girl named Morganna.

The Pie Place is a family restaurant. We adore children and encourage play and family fun. Don and Betchen first came to The Pie Place when their granddaughters were very young. They were reluctant to bring their rambunctious clan into to the restaurant, but we assured them that they – and the children – were very welcome.

We fell in love with the tiny, sweet faces of the girls immediately. Savita, extremely shy and with coal black eyes, held out her arms to be picked up. With her little arms clinging around my neck, it was love at first sight.

We make an exquisite radish dill soup, which is a customer favorite. Savita, a tentative eater, tried a cup. Four cups later, she declared it her favorite soup, too. Since then, they've sampled and enjoyed other favorite meals – part of learning and growing up.

As children do, the girls have grown. They are all in school now, and continue to come and eat with us whenever they come to stay at their grandparents' cabin. We are touched by the love that this family has showered on their tiny global family. We feel we are a special part of this family – and thanks be that we are counted as such by them.

Don and Betchen surrounded by their family. (photo by Erin Oberdorfer)

Painter's Vista Chicken Fruit Salad

This vibrant, colorful salad is perfect on a hot summer day. Reminiscent of spices found in the markets of India and the flavors of Don's early life there, curry, cloves, ginger and cinnamon are blended to create a zesty dressing. A simple, yet exotic salad that even young palates will appreciate.

Serves 4

Amount / Ingredients

Amount	Ingredients
1 pound	boneless, skinless chicken breasts, poached and sliced
2	navel oranges, peeled and separated into wedges
1 cup	seedless green grapes, halved
1 cup	seedless red grapes, halved
1 large head	Romaine lettuce, rinsed and torn into bite-sized pieces

Spicy Dressing

Amount	Ingredient
1 Tablespoon	Dijon mustard
1/4 cup	rice wine vinegar
2 Tablespoons	orange marmalade
1 Tablespoon	honey
1/2 cup	fresh mint leaves, stems removed
1/8 teaspoon	ground cloves
1/2 teaspoon	ground cinnamon
1 teaspoon	ground ginger
1 Tablespoon	mild curry powder
3/4 cup	peanut oil
1/4 cup	mustard oil (available at Indian grocery stores or substitute crushed, toasted mustard seeds in peanut oil)
	salt and freshly ground black pepper to taste

Instructions

To poach the chicken, arrange the skinless breasts in a pot large enough to fit them in one layer. Add water to completely cover the breasts 1/2 to 1 inch. Bring the liquid to a boil, reduce heat to low simmer with only an occasional bubble. Partly cover the pot, cook for about 10 minutes, then turn off the heat, leaving the chicken to finish cooking in the hot water for 10-15 more minutes.

Arrange torn Romaine lettuce on each plate. Build the salad by scattering the orange wedges along with the green and red grapes to best disperse the color of the fruit. Then fan the sliced chicken across the center top of the salad.

To prepare the dressing: In the bowl of a blender or food processor fitted with a steel blade, combine mustard, vinegar, marmalade, honey, mint, cloves, cinnamon, ginger and curry powder. Process 15 seconds or until smooth. With machine running, slowly drizzle in oils until thickened. Season with salt and pepper and chill until ready to serve. Drizzle dressing over the salad and serve.

DINNER THEATER

It seems to me that our three basic needs, for food, security and love are so mixed and mingled and inter-twined that we cannot straightly think of one without the others. So it happens that when I write of hunger, I am really writing about love and the hunger for it, and warmth and the love of it and the hunger for it … and then the warmth and richness and fine reality of hunger satisfied … and it is all one.
– from the Art of Eating by M.F.K. Fisher

When our family first came to Grand Marais, we lived in a little cabin clinging to the rocky shore of Lake Superior.

"Isolation Cabin," as we lovingly called it, was nestled among the trees. We spent many happy hours in that tiny dwelling engaged in conversation, creating and writing, cooking and admiring our surroundings.

One early summer day, we celebrated a birthday for Mary, one of our family members.

The surprise party involved a theatrical orchestration, creating a dining room among the birch and pines – a gauzy white tent billowing from branch to branch, appointed with wicker furniture and a white tablecloth laden with china, crystal and silverware.

Isolation Cabin is nestled among the trees near the Big Lake. (photo by Kathy Rice)

This was our view of Lake Superior from Isolation Cabin. (photo by Kathy Rice)

We painted a colorful wooden backdrop and performed a much-shortened version of "Much Ado About Nothing" on the weathered wooden deck of the cabin.

Though we lacked the old English accents, I believe Shakespeare would have applauded our heartfelt attempt.

In our diminutive kitchen (though the word "kitchen" seems too optimistic), we prepared a sumptuous five-course repast that in my memory remains one of the best ever tasted. Seated among her eager "chefs," Cheryl orchestrated the amazing score of dishes that she'd selected and we'd prepared together. Like a dance, we maneuvered within the confines of the tiny space to create a memorable meal and experience.

It was while we were having dessert and coffee that evening that our conversation turned to our dreams for the future.

"If we ever own a restaurant," said someone, "the warm potato, sausage and goat cheese salad would be great to serve!"

We didn't know then that dream would become a reality.

We've learned a lot about food since that birthday dinner years ago.

Cheryl devoured cookbooks, using their inspiration to create tasty and nurturing homecooked gourmet meals to feature at The Pie Place.

Crafting the menu as finely as the food, she shaped the words as only she could, like poetry. Her culinary descriptions made you want to try each one and certainly made our guests ask to please keep the menu to read even after they'd ordered. Cheryl's passion for food and her love of people led us to fashion a restaurant where customers feel like – and to us actually are – family.

As our guests so often tell us, "Your restaurant is like coming home for dinner."

That is one of the best heart-cheering compliments we can receive.

Cheryl taught us that food is only one way that we feed each other. So many ingredients go into preparing an extraordinary meal, but we at The Pie Place believe the first ingredient must always be love.

Warm Potato, Sausage & Goat Cheese Salad

Just as we do, you'll love this delicate, light and totally irresistible potato salad. A perfect accompaniment to a celebratory dinner or as an unexpected take on a traditional favorite, goat cheese adds a sweet and nutty flavor. Savory homemade sausages, by our local butcher, make this a salad hearty enough to serve as an entrée as well. If you don't have the luxury of obtaining homemade sausages, a sweet or spicy Italian sausage will work nicely.

Serves 6

Amount	Ingredients
1 pound	fresh sausages of your choice, such as sweet or spicy Italian or bratwurst salt
2 pounds	white, red or yellow-fleshed potatoes, unpeeled, well-scrubbed and cubbed, we often use fingerling potatoes, which are excellent, but use them whole

Dressing

1	shallot, finely chopped
1 clove	garlic, minced
5 Tablespoons	fresh parsley, chopped and divided
1 Tablespoon	fresh chives, chopped
1 teaspoon	fresh basil, chopped
1 teaspoon	Dijon mustard
1 Tablespoon	fresh lemon juice
3 Tablespoons	white wine vinegar
3/4 cup	olive oil
1/2 teaspoon	salt
1/4 teaspoon	freshly ground pepper
3/4 cup	crumbled goat cheese, we use Gjetost and love the sweet, nutty flavor
1 bunch	red leaf lettuce for garnish, we like organic field greens

Instructions

Preheat a broiler or prepare a fire in a charcoal grill. Place the sausages on a broiler pan or grill rack and broil or grill, turning to cook evenly, until done – about 10 minutes, depending upon the sausage. Let cool, then cut on the diagonal into 1-inch thick slices. Place in a bowl.

Meanwhile, fill a large pot three-fourths full with water and bring to a boil. Add salt to taste and boil the potatoes until tender, but slightly resistant when pierced – 25 to 30 minutes. Don't overcook! Drain and let cool slightly. Cut into 1-inch cubes and add to the sausages.

To make the dressing: In a small bowl, combine the shallot, garlic, 1 tablespoon of the parsley, chives, basil, mustard, lemon juice and vinegar. Whisk to mix well. Slowly drizzle the olive oil, in a thin stream, whisking continuously. Add salt and pepper to taste.

Pour the dressing over the potatoes and sausage and mix gently. Taste again for seasoning. Add the cheese and 2 tablespoons of the parsley and toss gently.

Line a serving dish with lettuce leaves and spoon the salad on top. Garnish with the remaining 2 tablespoons parsley and serve immediately.

"If we ever own a restaurant, the warm potato, sausage and goat cheese salad would be great to serve!"

ANGEL PIE

I will arise now and go, for always night and day.
I hear lake water lapping with low sounds by the shore.
– William Butler Yeats

A few weathered fish houses still cling to the rocky shore of Lake Superior, reminders of earlier days when commercial fishing sustained the lives of families who made their homes here on the mainland in Grand Marais or on the islands of Isle Royale.

They lived their lives with sun, wind and rain and with capable hands pulled heavy nets of herring onto the decks of their boats.

Tommy returns after a morning of fishing. (photo by Jon Vezner) His daughter MaryBeth Gilmer photographed him at the old fish house.

Many came from Norway and Sweden, living as their fathers had lived, close to the seas, catching the fish to sustain their families and the families of others.

Fishing families like the Sivertsons, the Toftes and the Eckels create a rich catch of stories about life as a commercial fisherman.

Tom Eckel was a legend and friend among many in Grand Marais. Fishing even after his retirement, Lake Superior was his constant companion.

Tom was a frequent visitor at the Pie Place, his love of sweets as strong as his love of the sweetwater sea.

One late afternoon he appeared, face sunburned and eyes sparkling, looking for an "angel pie."

"I had one once," he said with yearning. He explained a lemony, light delicacy as if he could taste it as he spoke.

I told him we didn't have an "angel pie," but since he had vacationed in Key West and had come to love Key lime pie, he should give ours a try.

He cocked his head with a doubtful grin, but took a slice, promising that he'd be back to let me know what he thought.

A few days later, he returned singing its praises and promptly asking for another piece. Thereafter, when he needed a "lift," up the hill he came for his favorite pie.

A few years ago, on a icy winter day, a runaway logging truck, whose brakes had failed, careened down the Gunflint Trail unable to stop. It crashed into Tommy's fish house, coming to rest in the harbor. Miraculously, the driver survived, but the beloved fish house did not. The historic building was gone.

A few days later, Tommy appeared looking exhausted and lost.

"Got any Key lime pie?" Of course we did.

True to the hardworking spirit of a fisherman, Tom collaborated with North House Folk School to assist in constructing a new fish house on the site of his original building. A beautiful timber-frame structure, it did Tom proud. Before long, he was happily cleaning herring in the fish house, while North House classes were being held in other parts of the large, rustic building.

One day while cleaning fish and talking animatedly, Tommy collapsed. He was rushed to the local hospital where he lay weak from the effects of congestive heart failure. We sent along a slice of Tommy's favorite pie to the hospital, and his sister Patty said he seemed a bit perkier that day.

Sadly, Tommy passed away a few weeks later. These days I like to think of him with that bemused twinkle, looking down on us and saying, "Finally had a piece of that Angel Pie, and it was mighty good."

And spending his time now with that fisher of men, Tommy must be feasting on some mighty fine fish, too.

Smoked Trout Paté

Grand Marais has a long history of commercial fishing, and nobody knew fish better than Tommy. I think this paté would do him proud. It's quick, easy and perfect for any occasion. We smoke our own fish, but you can purchase smoked fish at most fish markets. For a true taste of the North Shore, give this recipe a try. (Then have a slice of pie and think again about Tom.)

Makes 3 cups

Amount — Ingredients

Amount	Ingredients
1 pound	smoked trout fillet, skinned and deboned
4 ounces	cream cheese, room temperature
3 Tablespoons	unsalted butter, room temperature
2 Tablespoons	cognac, optional
2 Tablespoons	finely chopped red onion, plus more for garnish
1/2 teaspoon	Worcestershire sauce
1 Tablespoon	chopped fresh dill, plus more for garnish
2 teaspoons	fresh lemon juice
	Hot sauce, such as Tabasco, to taste
	Coarse salt and freshly ground pepper, to taste

Instructions

Purée trout, cream cheese, butter, cognac, onion, Worcestershire sauce and dill in a food processor. Add lemon juice, a few drops of hot sauce, salt and pepper – and pulse. Transfer to a bowl. Cover and refrigerate for at least 1 hour (or overnight). Garnish with more onion and dill and serve with crackers or sliced, toasted baguette.

THE CIRCLE

We love Grand Marais as a haven in a world where accusations often are flung like handfuls of sand against an unsuspecting face. Here people can be who they are without fear of reprisals.

Thus the town attracts a diversity of people with warm and giving spirits, full of humor, creativity and the best of what it means to be a spiritual being having a human experience. We are blessed to have all manner of friends who make our life, and the life of our local and global community, a better one.

We are not alone in appreciating the welcoming circle that surrounds our town.

Greg Anderson and his partner Will Tuthill split their time between New York and Grand Marais. Greg and I were chatting as he ate breakfast at the café one morning when he revealed, "Life hasn't always been easy for us. People can be very cruel. Grand Marais, and most of the people in the community, is very open. Will and I have felt accepted here and loved for the people we are."

Greg and Will's experiences made me remember the tragedy that befell another local couple whose lives brought joy and caring to the world.

Ken Peterson and Rob Burgess were both pediatric physicians who also divided their time between Gunflint Trail and another far-flung rural region. They served children in remote Alaskan villages for nearly 40 years. They were much loved in our community, too.

One recent evening, Ken was on the way back to his cabin at Seagull Lake after attending choir practice at the Lutheran church. A tree had fallen onto the Gunflint Trail, blocking passage. Generous of spirit like many of those who live in our beloved region, he stopped, took a chainsaw out of his truck and began to remove the obstacle. He was struck by a car and killed instantly.

After the sad accident, a letter featured in the *News Herald* from an Native Alaskan friend of the couple came to our attention. She cherished Ken and Rob for their skills and kindnesses. In the letter, the woman wrote, "Ken knew his God was a God of love who would never turn away from an expression of love as fine and as good as that which he shared with Rob."

She ended with a quote from the poem "Outwitted" by Edwin Markham. It is both poignant and beautiful. It is how we try to live our lives.

Greg and Will on the day they were married, October 16, 2011.
(photo courtesy Greg and Will)

"He drew a circle that shut me out,
Heretic, rebel, a thing to flout.
But love and I had wit to win,
We drew a circle that took him in."

Wild Blueberry Thyme Marsala Sorbet

Sorbet is simple to make, yet adds a festive panache to any meal. We make sorbets out of whatever fruit is fresh, flavorful and in season. We once made roasted corn and mustard sorbet to garnish our gazpacho; it was fantastic. Serve sorbet after soup and salad courses and before the main entrée as a palate cleanser. Present it in glass cups, garnished with fresh thyme and a flourish of blueberries. You may receive a standing ovation, as a table of enthusiastic guests once did us.

Serves 6

Amount   Ingredients

Amount	Ingredients
4 to 5 cups	fresh wild blueberries
3 Tablespoons	dry Marsala
2 Tablespoons	fresh lemon juice
1 pinch	salt

Thyme-infused Syrup

8 to 10	fresh thyme leaves
2 cups	sugar
1 cup	water
	cheesecloth bag will be needed

Instructions

In a stainless steel pot, cook the fresh wild blueberries, Marsala, lemon juice and salt until the berries soften and begin to burst, releasing their color and flavor. Stir occasionally. Purée when cool.

For the syrup: In a heavy pot, combine sugar and water. Tie the thyme leaves into a cheesecloth bag and add to the pot. Bring to a boil, stirring frequently until the sugar is completely dissolved. Remove from heat and let the thyme steep for 20 minutes. Remove thyme bag and cool.

Combine purée with simple syrup. Use 3/4 cup syrup for a slightly less sweet sorbet or 1 cup for a sweeter sorbet. Place mixture in a freezer-safe container and freeze until firm, about 3 hours.

Place a few small scoops of the sorbet in small, pretty glass cups or bowls.

GRANDFATHER'S BEANS

In the end we will conserve only what we love,
we will love only what we understand,
we will understand only what we are taught.
– Baba Dioum

Duane Hasegawa and Barb Heideman have a cabin in Grand Marais, nestled in the woods near our original Pie Place. They come to the North Shore as often as they can to seek the solace of towering pines and the Big Lake.

Duane, an avid gardener, shares our passion for fresh vine-ripened tomatoes, warmed by the sun and sweet in your mouth.

Because we live (happily so) in an area where summers are short and growing seasons even shorter, we've been on a quest to find a variety of tomatoes that will trick Mother Nature. We need a tomato plant that grows rapidly, ripening its ruby fruit before the first heavy frost.

Duane discovered a tomato plant more suitable to our northern climate and sent us seeds. We received and treasured them like a gift from the Magi.

One day when Duane and Barb were in for lunch, the conversation turned to gardening, hardy seed types, and Seed Savers Exchange, an incredible company that gathers heirloom seeds and has saved them. Some of the seeds are more than 100 years old.

Duane had his own story of saving seeds. While sorting through some things that had belonged to his grandfather in Japan, he came upon an old jar filled with beans. Duane remembered his grandfather out planting beans and tending his garden. His grandfather prized beans and always planted them to be an essential component of each season's harvest.

I imagined vines winding up bamboo trellises, green tendrils unfurling like fingers reaching for the sun.

Year after year, he gathered his beans, and at the end of harvest time, beans were dried and saved to ensure a new bounty for the coming year.

Duane in the top photo tends beans descended from his grandfather's garden in Japan in the bottom photo. (U.S. photo by Barb Heideman)

Finding the beans, Duane felt compelled to carry on his grandfather's garden legacy and planted them among his other varieties, eager to see if they would grow.

Despite their age, the beans took hold in the warm, rich soil and began to sprout.

As Duane recounted the story of his grandfather's passion for gardening and for his beans, it became clear that time and distance do not truly exist between us. Whether here and now in our northern forest or many, many years ago in Japan, those beans spanned time, reconnecting through the simple joy of a garden, the smell of freshly turned earth and the feel of rich soil sifting through your fingers.

These things connect us to each other and to our ancestors. They remind us that we are stewards of a great and wondrous gift.

Green Beans with Caramelized Onion

Those hot, lazy days of summer should be savored in so many ways – a refreshing swim in the Lake, a picnic under the cool shade of a tree and a harvest from a lush garden. Summer is a favorite time to bring fresh produce to our restaurant table. Like Duane's grandfather, we love fresh green beans and this recipe will bring the taste of summer to your table.

Serves 8

Amount / Ingredients

Amount	Ingredients
2 pounds	fresh green beans
2 large	sweet onions
3 Tablespoons	butter
3 Tablespoons	light brown sugar
1-1/2 Tablespoons	balsamic vinegar

Instructions

Trim beans. Cook beans in boiling water to cover 12 to 15 minutes or until tender. Drain and set aside or cover and chill overnight if desired. Meanwhile, cut onions into thin slices and cut each slice in half.

Melt 1 tablespoon butter in a large nonstick skillet over medium-high heat, and add onion. Cook 8 to 10 minutes (do not stir). Continue cooking onion, stirring often, 15 to 20 minutes or until golden. Reduce heat to medium. Stir in remaining 2 tablespoons of butter and brown sugar.

Add green beans and cook 5 minutes or until thoroughly heated. Add vinegar; toss to coat.

DOLLE AND HAN

Picture this: It's the Fourth of July and we're sitting high above our little town of Grand Marais on Pincushion Overlook, watching the harbor. A chill has rolled in off Lake Superior, but we're wrapped in blankets, snug and warm.

"Pass the popcorn down this way," someone says. "The fireworks are about to start!"

Our patriotic companions and fellow popcorn munchers are Holle and Dan Despen. From the Twin Cities, they've been coming to Grand Marais and to The Pie Place for, well, it seems like forever.

We share many of the same interests – sailing, art (Holle and I could talk for hours), Asian food (Dan adores our sushi), kayaking, and generally enjoying life in our North Shore home.

So, on this particular July Fourth, after breakfast at The Pie Place, Dan and Holle invited us to join them to take in the local display of fireworks (which for a small town is pretty spectacular) and for banter, lots of popcorn and even more laughter.

Holle and Dan love giving things … beautiful handmade cards, awesome rubber stamps, books, and their knowledge and shared passions from Japanese tea ceremonies to sailing – you name it.

Last year our waiter Jeremy became the proud owner of a Snipe, a small but racy little sailboat. Dan, a sailor himself, noted a part that needed repair. He took it home, fixed and painted it, and returned secretly to install the now shiny red and good-as-new splash. (If like me, you're not up on sailboats, it's the thing that keeps the water from splashing into your face.)

One summer day, busy and scurrying from one table to the next, I saw Holle and Dan coming in the front door.

I got so excited that I exclaimed, "Dolle and Han are here!" I didn't realize my mistake until they burst out laughing. From that day forward, they became "Dolle and Han" to us.

But truly, they don't mind … as long as our head chef Josh remembers to give Holle extra jam with her biscuits and gravy!

Dan, Holle and Kayce enjoy a few quiet moments at the cabin. (photo by Deborah Steenbakker)

Raspberry Rhubarb Jam

Homemade jam is one of the things that Holle loves. We love all kinds of jams, often making them based on our pies – blueberry sour cherry, blackberry peach and raspberry rhubarb jam. It doesn't get much better than the marriage of sweet, plump raspberries and the tartness of rhubarb to make the perfect jam.

Makes 9 jars (8 ounces) of jam

Amount / Ingredients

Amount	Ingredients
3 pounds	rhubarb, fresh or frozen
3 cups	sugar
1/2 cup	water
2 cups	raspberries, fresh or frozen

Instructions

Cut rhubarb into 1/2 inch pieces and combine with raspberries. Add water and sugar.

Cook mixture in a heavy pot, stirring frequently to prevent scorching, for 30 minutes, or until jam begins to thicken.

Put in sterile jam jars and seal in a water bath according to Sure Jell canning directions. There is no need to use pectin in this particular jam, as the rhubarb has its own natural pectin (as is the case with tart fruit such as crab apples and lingonberries).

If you plan on eating the jam within a reasonable amount of time (a month or two), it may be stored safely in the refrigerator.

A Spot of Tea

We adore the Reynolds crew!

Their family, some of whom were born in South Africa, fill the restaurant with the warmth and laughter of a close-knit clan.

They've frequented The Pie Place for many years. As a result, we've had the joy-filled opportunity to see the children emerge into young people with diverse and tremendous personalities.

When the Reynolds family arrives, the room brims with five children and an entourage of friends. (I'd want to spend time with their family, too!).

A tea party atmosphere ensues ... the whole gang loves tea, from the youngest, Daniel and Chloe, to the older kids, Nina, Ian and Michael. In true English (and South African) fashion, they drink pot after pot of tea. Sometimes they heap it with sugar (right, Michael?). The room fills with happy chatter and laughter that captures even those of us working.

Coming myself from a family of English/Irish tea drinkers, where a pot of strong black tea was served at the end of our evening meal, I can understand their enthusiasm for the beverage. There's something convivial about the experience of sharing tea.

The Reynolds family, as you might expect, love our scones, too. However, don't be fooled ... these young people have a seasoned palate, eating everything from our classic Caesar salad to crab cakes. Young Daniel loves sushi and shares my taste for fresh-made Caesar dressing.

Is it any wonder that when the Reynolds arrive, we all feel like we've joined the party and are part of their moveable festivities.

The Reynolds clan, from left Ian, Michael, Daniel, Nina, Chloe, Jonathan and Marja. (photo by Jeremy Chase)

Caesar Dressing with Romaine Salad

When I turned 16, my parents took me to dinner at the Roosevelt Hotel in Lansing, Michigan. The restaurant was a darkly paneled, candle-lit space with crisp white linen tablecloths and napkins and a roaring fire in the stone fireplace. It seemed to me the height of elegance. I remember, as vividly as if it were yesterday, our waiter making the Caesar dressing tableside, rubbing the large wooden bowl with fresh garlic and whisking in the lemon juice and amber olive oil. He tore the crisp romaine leaves by hand, tossed in large handmade croutons and drizzled the salad with the fresh dressing. Since then, I have been a Caesar salad devotee. Some day I'll show young Daniel Reynolds how to make his favorite dressing. I've tweaked this version to my tastes over the years – maybe more parsley, another clove of garlic or a titch – as Grandma said – more lemon juice. Experiment and find your own favorite flavor of this classic.

Makes about 1 quart

Amount / Ingredients

Amount	Ingredients
2 large cloves	garlic, minced
1 can (2-ounce size)	anchovy fillets packed in oil, drained and blotted with paper towel, we like King Oscar brand
3 teaspoons	Dijon mustard
1/4 cup	fresh parsley, chopped
1-1/2 teaspoons	Worcestershire sauce
6 Tablespoons	lemon juice
3	raw eggs, extreme care must be taken with raw eggs in handling and use, some may prefer to use pasteurized eggs
3/4 teaspoon	black pepper
3/4 cup	freshly grated Parmesan cheese, preferably Parmigiano-Reggiano
2 cups	olive oil
	Romaine lettuce, enough for the number of salads you'll prepare

Instructions

In the bowl of blender or food processor fitted with a steel blade, combine garlic, anchovies, mustard, parsley, Worcestershire sauce, lemon juice, eggs, pepper and Parmesan cheese. Process 30 seconds or until smooth.

With machine running, slowly drizzle in oil in a thin stream. Be sure not to overbeat or dressing will become too thick.

This recipe makes about a quart of dressing but should be used quickly – within a week – and kept refrigerated because of the eggs. Make less dressing if you think you'll have too much. However, if you are planning a party and want to serve a group of 10 to 12 people, plan on using most of it.

Romaine leaves should always be torn and not cut. When tossing in the dressing, leaves should be adequately covered, but not too wet. Once dressed, your Caesar salads should be served immediately to avoid wilting.

Always Room at Our Table

Thanksgiving has grown to be a particularly festive occasion at The Pie Place. We come together to prepare traditional fare. When our guests arrive, it's like our family coming home.

"Over the river and through the woods" is a reality in our North Woods home. Guests travel from afar to join in our celebration. Of course, our guests don't travel in horse-drawn sleighs, wrapped in woolen blankets against the winter's chill, but they often endure icy, snow-covered roads to arrive at our door.

Traditional foods, with sprinkles of the North Woods, grace our holiday table. Succulent roast turkey, glazed with fresh-pressed apple cider and local maple syrup, is stuffed with wild rice and mushrooms. Mounds of fluffy mashed potatoes are swaddled in rich, savory gravy. Squash casserole the color of a fall pumpkin patch and homemade cranberry sauce delight the taste buds and, not to be forgotten, is the pumpkin pie with fresh whipped cream. Ah, tradition!

"The Pie Place doesn't seem like a restaurant," one guest said. "It feels like coming home for Thanksgiving!" That's about the best compliment we can receive … and this gathering of people sharing warmth and gratitude is home.

Many couples and families return year after year, making it their tradition. Many guests have gotten acquainted with each other from past Thanksgivings. They call in advance to ask, "Are Terry and Ila coming? Then we'll be coming, too!"

It's always festive … cedar boughs, pumpkins and squashes for decorations; greetings, laughter and lots of hugs for the entertainment.

Happy Thanksgiving - Buddy style. (photo by Denny Fitzpatrick)

People tell us they regret that we have to work on Thanksgiving, but it doesn't seem like work to us. We bake squash, stuff turkeys and put the finishing touches on the "autumnal vignettes" that grace our tables – all in joyful anticipation of the arrival of our Pie Place family and friends.

One year, Buddy, a devoted employee and longtime friend, was leaving Grand Marais with his sister, Maryl, and brother-in-law, Denny, to spend the holiday with family out of town. As usual, they stopped at The Pie Place to pick up their Thanksgiving pies. Soon after, it started snowing heavily – a soft, beautiful, muffled snow that painted everything frosty and white. It was a visual fairyland, but made travel treacherous for some.

An hour or so after Buddy and his family left, I heard our chef Josh say, "Buddy, Maryl and Denny are back!" They appeared at the front door, weary and covered with snow.

"The roads are a glare of ice," explained Maryl, "so we turned around and came back. Do you have room for us?"

Of course we did. The Pie Place shares the philosophy of my grandmother: "There's always room for another at my table."

Spiced Cranberry Sauce

Thanksgiving dinner at The Pie Place wouldn't be complete without our friends, turkey and cranberry sauce. We love this slightly different take on a traditional favorite. Fresh pears and ginger root add spice to our sauce.

Makes 2-1/2 cups

Amount · Ingredients

Amount	Ingredients
1 cup	water
1 cup	sugar
1 piece (about 3 inches)	fresh ginger, peeled
1	firm ripe pear, diced, we prefer Bosc pears
1 teaspoon	grated lemon rind
1 package (12-ounce size)	fresh or frozen cranberries
2 Tablespoons	fresh lemon juice

Instructions

Bring water, sugar and ginger to a boil in a heavy saucepan, stirring constantly for 15 minutes. Add pear and lemon rind. Return mixture to a boil and cook, stirring occasionally for 3 minutes. Stir in cranberries. Reduce heat and simmer without stirring for 3 to 5 minutes or until cranberries pop. Remove from heat; cool. Remove ginger. Cover and chill.

Sauce can be chilled up to 2 days. Stir in lemon juice just before serving.

"The Pie Place doesn't feel like a restaurant. . . . It feels like coming home for Thanksgiving."

Recipe Notes

Recipe Notes

Welcome to

Sweetgrass
Cove

RETREAT FOR BODY MIND
ON LAKE SUPERIOR

Sandwiches &
Savoring The Season

BUDDY

Buddy enjoys time in the garden amid the colors and beauty.
(photo by Jeremy Chase)

Buddy Skinner works with us at The Pie Place. Young in so many ways no matter what his age, his is the childlike presence who weaves simple, yet profound truths into the fabric of our life.

Buddy loves music. He can sing the words to just about any song you'd like to hear. All day long, he loves singing happily at the top of his lungs as he goes about his tasks. Buddy is sunshine and laughter.

A willing worker, Buddy fills his days with folding pie boxes, feeding the birds, sweeping the floor, watering the flowers (and sometimes the rocks) and singing with our Old English sheepdog, Willoughby. They are fast friends.

He loves nothing more than to hear the words: "Buddy, we need you! Could you please clear the tables on the porch for us?" Energetically he swings into action, clearing the remnants of a lunch in a flash.

We all need to be needed, to feel that we are being of service, to know that we make a vital difference in others' lives and to be a part of something bigger. In this way, Buddy reflects all of us.

Buddy goes through his life doing those things that fill him with a sense of worth and belonging. He is truly a member of The Pie Place family.

And so when he smiles at a customer coming in for lunch or a pie and says, "Welcome to our Pie Place," his words are true.

"He spends his days singing happily at the top of his lungs as he goes about his tasks."

Grilled Peanut Butter & Banana Split Sandwich

Remember sitting cross-legged under the trees on a warm summer day, eating the perfect peanut butter and jelly sandwich? In my mind's eye, I still see the grape jelly, glistening purple in the sun, as it squished out the sides of the soft, white bread and onto my hands. My first puppy, a beagle, was named Skippy and I don't remember if the dog or my brand preference for the peanut butter came first.

Many of us retain that child inside who relished those PB&J sandwiches. Here's a "grown-up" twist on a traditional childhood favorite. I think our moms would approve and Buddy does, too.

Serves 1

Amount — Ingredients

Amount	Ingredients
2	slices firm white sandwich bread, divided
1 teaspoon	butter, softened
1 Tablespoon	creamy peanut butter (or crunchy, if you're a fan)
2 teaspoons	honey
6 or so	semisweet chocolate mini-chips, or more to your taste
1 large	strawberry, thinly sliced
1/2 small	banana, cut lengthwise into 3 slices (about 2 ounces)
1 Tablespoon	pineapple jam

Instructions

Spread 1 side of each white bread slice with 1/2 teaspoon butter. Combine peanut butter and honey; spread over plain side of 1 bread slice. Sprinkle with chocolate chips; top evenly with strawberry slices and banana slices.

Spread pineapple jam over plain side of remaining bread slice. Carefully assemble sandwich with buttered sides out.

Heat a small nonstick skillet over medium-high heat. Add sandwich, cook 2 minutes on each side or until lightly browned.

Sit under your favorite tree … and enjoy.

Dish-pan Hands

Rarely in the history of restaurants does one experience a customer who joyfully wants to do dishes after a meal.

Sounds like a hallucination? No, it is absolutely true.

It all started with pie.

Steve and Rosemary Hartman have been coming to the North Shore for years, staying at Hollow Rock, their favorite lodging near Grand Marais. They always would stop at The Pie Place on their way to the cabin to pick up a blueberry pie, Steve's favorite.

Two years ago, after lingering over a delicious breakfast and a second cup of coffee, I jokingly told Steve, "Our dishwasher didn't come in today (true!). How'd you like to do dishes?" Then I think I laughed at my own joke.

Steve's eyes lit up. "Sure! I would love to do dishes!"

"Yeah, sure you would," I laughed some more.

Then Rosemary chimed in. "No, he really does love doing dishes. Besides, I want to go shopping for a couple of hours, and it would be great to get him out of my hair for awhile."

My "No really, I was only joking" was totally ignored. Rosemary headed out the front door, a smile on her face, and Steve grabbed his coffee and an apron and headed for the kitchen.

In our pancake-flipping kitchen, breakfast was in full swing. Steve pulled a bright red bandana from his back pocket, shook it out with a flair and tied it around his forehead – ready for action.

He kept us in stitches all morning long, drinking coffee, telling jokes, giving our chef Josh (the master egg cooker) hints on egg etiquette, and in the midst of it all doing stacks (and I mean stacks) of dishes with graceful efficiency. He was as happy as the proverbial clam, if clams loved to do dishes.

Imagine my surprise when at the end of his "shift," he thanked me for "letting him do dishes."

I like to imagine his surprise when they found a freshly baked blueberry pie in the back seat of their car.

Then this last summer who should appear at our kitchen door with an eager smile on his face?

You got it. The guy with the dish-pan hands.

"I'm reporting for my shift," Steve said playfully. "Need a good dishwasher?"

And guess what, our dishwasher hadn't shown up that day.

I'd call that Divine Providence … or the universe making happiness for one dishwashing-crazy clam.

Steve and Rosemary at Lake Superior shore near Hollow Rock. (photo courtesy the Hartmans)

Hollow Rock Sandwich

In homage to Hollow Rock, the rocky arch in Lake Superior, we created this artfully layered sandwich, full of texture and flavor. Once you taste this delightful sandwich, it will have a favored place on your table as well.

Makes 6

Amount — Ingredients

Amount	Ingredients
1/2 cup	mayonnaise, we prefer Hellmann's
2 Tablespoons	chopped fresh tarragon
2 Tablespoons	chopped fresh Italian parsley
1/4 cup	curry powder (if you prefer less spice, reduce curry by half)
2 Tablespoons	ground cumin
1-1/2	jalapeño chilies, seeded and minced
2 teaspoons	salt, divided, 1 for spice mix, 1 for seasoning chicken
1 teaspoon	ground cloves
6 Tablespoons	olive oil
2 large	white onions, thinly sliced
2 large	tart green apples (such as Granny Smith) cored, sliced, leave peel on
6	boneless chicken breast halves
	salt and pepper, to taste
12 slices	whole grain bread

Instructions

Stir mayonnaise, tarragon and parsley in small bowl to blend; this can be made ahead and refrigerated. In a separate bowl, mix the curry, cumin, chilies, 1 teaspoon of salt and cloves.

Heat 4 tablespoons olive oil in heavy large skillet over medium heat. Add onions and 2 tablespoons spice mixture and sauté 10 minutes. Reduce heat to medium-low and sauté until onions are very tender and golden brown, stirring frequently, about 25 minutes. Transfer onions to bowl and cool. Cover and refrigerate.

Heat 1 tablespoon oil in same skillet over medium-high heat. Toss apples with 2 tablespoons spice mixture. Add to skillet and sauté until apples are crisp but tender, about 5 minutes. Transfer to another bowl and cool.

Preheat your oven broiler. Season chicken with the remaining salt and pepper. Brush with remaining 1 tablespoon oil. Broil chicken until cooked through, about 4 minutes on a side. Transfer chicken to work surface. Cut diagonally into 1/4-inch thick slices.

Spread herb mayonnaise on 1 side of each bread slice. Arrange apples, onion and chicken on 6 bread slices, dividing equally. Top with remaining bread slices. Cut in half and serve.

A Cove Where
Sweet Grass Grows

There are places on the North Shore so special and so memorable that they inspire us to create a recipe or dish honoring them. Hence the Sweet Grass Cove Chicken Sandwich, which has become a customer favorite at The Pie Place.

Sweet Grass Cove is a fabulous spa retreat, owned and operated by Rick Anderson and his beloved dog, Ruby. Situated on the rocky Lake Superior shore and nestled among the trees, it is truly heaven on earth. They say that God is in the details and being pampered by Rick, with his attention to every nuance, is heavenly.

Warm terrycloth robes, a steamy, oil-scented sauna, a hot tub surrounded by trees and with a fantastic view of the Big Lake, a roaring fire beside which you can curl up with herbal tea and a good book after a massage … well, need I say more?

We were charmed on our first visit to Sweet Grass Cove when Rick served us a beautiful, fresh and healthy lunch. Don't let the word "healthy" fool you into thinking "drab." This gourmet lunch featuring wild-nettle crêpes wrapped around succulent chicken breasts and fresh asparagus would have

Sweet Grass Cover nestles along the shore. Rick and Lucy, his first spa dog, hike to Mount Josephine. (photos by Kathy Rice)

made Jacques Pepin proud. One sure way to restaurateurs' hearts is to cook for them, to give them the luxury of savoring a meal prepared by someone else.

Calming your mind, flowing with the rhythm of the day, resting, soaking, breathing in the cool sweetness of fresh air, listening to the sounds of birds overhead and to the wind blowing through the pines – these nourish and restore you mind, body and soul, and this is what Rick's haven allows you to do.

After that first delicious day, we sat with Rick, munching aged Gouda, sipping crisp white wine and talking until the sun went down. The seeds of friendship had been planted.

Fragrant sweet grass grows at Sweet Grass Cove, and friendship grows there, too.

Sweet Grass Cove Roasted Chicken Sandwich

Beautiful, energizing and memorable, we pay homage to Rick and his haven. This gourmet merging of flavors will make you want to return to this sandwich again and again.

Serves 4

Amount / Ingredients

Amount	Ingredients
8 slices	multigrain bread, use your favorite, we use our homemade wild rice oatmeal bread
	mayonnaise, for spreading, we like Hellmann's
1-1/4 cups	homemade cranberry sauce (or a 14-ounce can whole cranberries)
2 large	split chicken breasts with bone-in and skin-on, roasted and sliced
	olive oil to rub chicken
2	Hass avocados, pitted and sliced
	salt and pepper, to taste
4 leaves	Romaine lettuce, cleaned and patted dry

Instructions

To roast chicken, rub the breasts with oil and cook on baking sheet in preheated 375° F oven for 20 to 30 minutes, turning over breasts after about 10 minutes. Roasting with the skin and bone is more flavorful than boneless, skinless breasts.

To assemble sandwich, lay out slices of bread and spread a layer of mayonnaise and whole cranberry sauce over each slice to desired thickness. Evenly cover entire slice of bread with sliced chicken and avocado, sprinkle lightly with salt and pepper and add crisp lettuce. Enjoy!

So Many Books, So Little Time

Situated on the old John Beargrease Road and facing the Big Lake sits a cluster of tiny cabins owned in the early days of commercial fishing by Nels Norman. Nels, a hardy Norwegian, built his cabins in Hovland and fished from the craggy Lake Superior shore. He and his fellow fishermen were known as "herring chokers" (I'll leave that to your imagination, since food is involved here) and those hardy, freshwater seafaring men made their living in this way.

Then, as now, it was the custom for fisherfolk to rent out cabins for additional income, a perfect pastime for fishermen's wives. Nels' wife took on the task with exuberance, adding to the long list of duties expected of a North Shore woman.

Only a few of these historic and charming landmarks remain. Years ago, Chuck and Helen Faust purchased three of Nels' cabins, merging two to create a cozy retreat and turning the third into an art studio and guest cabin. Today, nearly a century after these herring chokers put down their nets, Chuck and Helen are perfect stewards of the Norman legacy.

Literary and creative people by nature, they have lovingly restored and tended the Norman home and continue to keep Nels' story alive.

One sunny summer day, I was invited to Chuck and Helen's cabin. As a couple who, like me, relish a great story, they wove a tale of this fisherman's life. Between sips of strong and aromatic coffee, which I think Nels would have greatly savored, they recounted the events that characterize a life lived hard and well. They feel at home in Nels' house and I think he would have enjoyed their company.

Nels' cabin has been lovingly restored and enjoyed by Chuck, Helen, family and friends. (photo by Kathy Rice)

In our quest to prepare meals that are fresh and flavorful, we at The Pie Place go to the market each day to select fresh fruits and vegetables, meats and fish. Brown paper bags are filled to the brim, heavy with the purchases of the day.

Other great things also come in brown paper bags. Chuck and Helen, fellow lovers of words, bring us bags of books and more books.

They savor food and words in equal measure, and over the years, their meals in the restaurant have been seasoned with literary conversations and recommendations.

"You'll fall in love with him, such a soulful writer" or "One of my favorite books" and "This one will bring you to your knees."

One summer day, Chuck and Helen's grandson, Chad, then age 9, eagerly presented me with a book list. "You have to read *A Wrinkle in Time*, you'll just love it!"

I take book suggestions most seriously, and assured him it would be on my winter reading list.

It's not uncommon for Chuck, an apple pie lover, to poke his head through the kitchen door and proclaim with a mischievous grin, "What's a guy need to do to get a pie around here?"

Thus, a great opportunity to hold him ransom: "You suggest a good book, and we'll give you a pie."

Seems to work out pretty well, and much to our delight, they keep coming back with great appetites for food and for books.

Loon's Song Ham Panini

This memorable sandwich, served hot with our Curried Acorn Squash & Apple Soup (see page 29), makes a perfect meal with which to curl up and read a good book. Our Cheryl Polson, creator of the sandwich, named it for one of her favorite North Woods sounds – the call of the loons.

Serves 4

Chuck & Helen relax at their cabin. (photo by Kathy Rice)

Amount	Ingredients
12 ounces	maple honey-baked ham, sliced
16-ounce round	Brie, peeled
1/2 cup	strawberry jam
3 Tablespoons	melted butter
8 slices	French bread

Instructions

While your panini iron is pre-heating, lay out French bread slices and brush one side with melted butter, using a pastry brush. Flip bread over and spread on strawberry jam. Place Brie on other side, layer with slices of ham, then Brie again. (The cheese on each side will melt and function like glue to hold the sandwich together.) Place in panini iron and grill until golden brown.

If you don't own a panini iron, you can achieve the same effect using a heavy-bottomed pan or well-seasoned cast-iron skillet. Place your sandwich in the skillet over medium heat, covered with a lid. When the bottom side turns golden brown, flip the sandwich over until the other side is also golden brown. If needed, add a bit more butter to the pan.

Bedtime Stories

Family – it's a warm, cozy word, like a blanket wrapped snugly around your shoulders. It conjures images of homemade, fresh-from-the-oven cookies, of people big and small sharing dinner around a large oak table, and, for many of us, of a father reading bedtime stories to an eager flock of pajama-clad children. It's ice skating on a frozen pond, and steamy hot cocoa afterward ("She got more marshmallows than I did!"), Christmas plays that only a parent could extol as Broadway material, and the work of eager young Picassos exhibited with pride on the family fridge.

Family is what The Pie Place is all about, and we love to hear our customers' family traditions.

Ed and Maud Joesting have been Pie Place friends for years. We've come to know their children and grandchildren and have witnessed their strength of a love and life shared.

Ed and Maud would come for lunch once or twice a week, truly as regular as clockwork. Ed was always gentlemanly and sweet, pulling out Maud's chair for her, helping her off and on with her coat. It was touching to see such love expressed after 60 years of marriage.

Sadly, in the final years of her life, Maud suffered from dementia. Ed, the love of her life, continued to be her vital link to everything and everyone around her.

Each time they came for lunch, she would say with tenderness, "We've been married for 60 years, and I love him as much today as I did when we were first married."

I would listen to her, as if hearing it for the first time. We never grow tired of hearing words of love. When Maud passed away, Ed was at her side, as he had been in life.

A man of strength and great faith, Ed began to live a life without his beloved Maud, and his children came to visit frequently, giving him solace, companionship and love.

Maud and Ed by Lake Superior. (photo by Lynn Day)

His daughter, Lynn, visits from Washington, and we enjoy one another. We share a passion for tea and eagerly exchange tea samples. The bond of tea and our mutual love for Ed have drawn us together.

One day this fall when Lynn was visiting her father, they came in for lunch. As they were leaving, I asked them what they were going to do for the evening.

"Dad is reading a book to me," Lynn said. "He read to us every night when we were young, all of us sitting on the floor around him. I loved to sit right next him. The words of the story would wash over me. It was so comforting. He still reads to me, and after all these years I still sit on the floor right by him."

There were tears in her eyes … and in my eyes, too. Not tears of sadness, but ones of gratitude and love for this man who gave the gift of stories.

Ed has since passed on, but I think Lynn would agree that her father also gave her another gift – the gift of family, someone to lean on, in childhood and adulthood.

And we should never be too grown-up for that.

North Shore Monte Cristo

This double-decker sandwich is a cross between breakfast and lunch, the egg batter-dipped and grilled bread is reminiscent of French toast. We've kicked ours up a notch by adding applewood-smoked bacon, Dijon mustard and our blueberry sour cherry jam. Dip the sandwich wedges in warm maple syrup and settle in for a cozy afternoon of reading with your family or friends.

Serves 1

Amount / Ingredients

Amount	Ingredients
2 large	eggs
1/4 cup	milk
1 pinch	salt
3 slices	firm bread, we use our homemade honey white
3 Tablespoons	butter
3 Tablespoons	blueberry sour cherry jam, or substitute any blueberry jam
2 slices	smoked turkey, from the deli
2 slices	applewood-smoked bacon, cooked slightly crisp
1 teaspoon	Dijon mustard
2 slices	sweet maple ham, from the deli
1 slice	Swiss cheese
	maple syrup, we prefer the local Wild Country brand

Instructions

Beat together eggs, milk and a pinch of salt. Then soak bread lightly in egg mixture.

Melt butter in a heavy skillet over medium-high heat. Cook the egg-soaked bread as you would French toast, until golden brown on each side, about 3 to 4 minutes.

Spread the jam on one side of two slices of bread. Layer smoked turkey and applewood-smoked bacon between the two (jam sides facing in). On the top bread, spread a layer of Dijon mustard, maple ham, Swiss cheese and then finish with a final slice of bread. (It's a double decker.) Return to frying pan and heat through until cheese melts.

Cut sandwich in an X to create four small triangles. These smaller pieces look pretty on the plate and make dipping into maple syrup a bit easier.

Serve with warmed maple syrup and a side of blueberry sour cherry jam.

LIBERATION

We came to know Bill and Angie Murray in bits and pieces … or perhaps it was "bites" and pieces. They'd come for dinner, almost always stayed for pie.

Between bites, a conversation would unfold, seasoned with a little of this and a little of that. It was meaty "life philosophy" talk or conversation about art, food and their days of snowshoeing and taking pictures along snow-laden trails.

A painted portrait of Bill by Tim Eling.

Bill, an artist and teacher extraordinaire, taught art at Stillwater Maximum Correctional Facility for 35 years.

As we came to know him, he talked a great deal about prison life, his students at Stillwater and the transformative power of art. Art provides inmates a way of expressing inner thoughts and feelings … of reaching out to a world barred to them during incarceration.

For the inmates, art connects them with their children and family members and gives them an opportunity to see a positive reflection of themselves and a sense of pride in what they can accomplish. Art offers a way to climb up the ladder to wholeness. As one inmate so poignantly put it, "Art literally saved my life."

As a result of meeting Bill, we've become involved, from afar, with his students. For 10 years, we've helped to get much needed art supplies for his classroom.

In return, we've been gifted with examples of their art, works that reveal their voice and express their gratitude. It teaches us how important it is that people do not feel alone and that they know others in the world see and care about them.

Bill gave a lecture one winter evening at the Grand Marais Art Colony titled "Prison Art."

As we stood before various paintings, we felt humbled by the expressions in paint and ink on canvas. Voices were heard without speaking. Stories were told brush stroke by brush stroke. Through the contemplative art, we looked into the hearts of those we'd come to see as friends.

Years have passed, Bill and Angie still come for dinner and our conversation remains as savory as ever.

Though Bill has retired from Stillwater, our relationship endures with those in prison who have touched our lives so profoundly.

Food does have a way of bringing people together, bridging even distance and life experiences.

Snowshoe Grill

Bill and Angie warm up with this sandwich after a morning of snowshoeing and taking photographs, and this scrumptious sandwich can battle a chilly winter day.

Serves 4

Amount / Ingredients

Amount	Ingredients
1 can (14-ounce size)	cherry pie filling
1/8 teaspoon	nutmeg
4 ounces	softened butter
8 slices	homemade honey white bread or any good quality white bread
8 to 12 slices	honey-baked ham, from the deli
6 ounces	Jarlsberg cheese

Instructions

In a small mixing bowl, stir nutmeg and cherry pie filling. Butter one side of each slice of bread. Turn buttered side down and spread cherry mixture on the other side of four slices. Divide ham and place on each sandwich along with sliced Jarlsberg cheese. Place remaining bread slices on top, buttered side on the outside. Grill sandwich as you would a grilled cheese, until golden brown and cheese has melted. Cut in half to serve.

Bill and Angie by their favorite Great Lake. (photo by Kathy Rice)

A Friend Along the Road

In her 80s, Millie Johnson personifies the eternal fountain of youth.

Spunky and full of life, her face beams as she shares her insights of the day, each one wrought from years of living and loving.

Millie is a member of the Johnson family, who own and operate the local grocery store. Despite our small town's remote location, the store is complete with a butcher whose expertise provides us with savory cuts of meat for our menu. It is a friendly and helpful place, like the grocery stores of old. Here you meet friends and exchange the happenings of the day, while searching through the fresh produce or selecting cans from the shelf.

Millie and I came to know each other when I did the daily excursions to the market.

As is the case in any family business, everyone pitches in to help when there's work to be done at the grocery. Often, on early mornings when I went to the grocery store, Millie was already there placing cans neatly on the shelves.

I always stopped for a few moments of conversation. Comrades through this daily communing, the span of years do not matter for Millie and me.

Millie starts from home. (photo by Kathy Rice)

Millie loves to walk, still putting in three miles a day, no matter the weather. Rain, snow or shine, she hikes along Highway 61, waving at everyone who passes by.

Millie told me a great story about her walks, and a friend she unknowingly made along the road.

Large freight trucks constantly pass through Grand Marais, carrying paper pulp from Thunder Bay to Duluth and cities beyond.

One day Millie, on her usual route, walked past one stopped truck from which emerged a ruddy-cheeked driver. He introduced himself and asked her name.

The stranger said that a truck driver's life is a lonely one, with miles of road and no one to talk to. He told her that he looked forward to seeing her, anticipating her presence along the roadside, her friendly wave warming his otherwise monotonous day.

Other truck drivers, too, he said, comment about Millie and how her friendliness meant a lot to them. She had become a bit of a legend among her trucker friends whom she hadn't met.

Millie was amazed at the difference made by her simple act.

"Can you believe it means so much to them? They honk at me now whenever they pass by."

"Connection is what we all long for," I agreed. "What seems like a small gesture can make a big difference in someone else's life."

Then I added, "You make a difference, Millie, to them and to me."

Angels come in many forms. They remind us that kindness is among the most important gifts we can give to one another.

Sometimes angels walk along the roadside, smiling and waving as they go.

The highway Millie walks along runs near the harbor downtown. (photo by Paul L. Hayden)

*"Can you believe it means so much to them?
They honk at me now
whenever they pass by."*

Asparagus, Poached Egg, Prosciutto & Fontina Cheese

Fresh asparagus, poached eggs, and prosciutto … some of our favorites co-mingle to create this simple, yet flavorful open-face sandwich. A perfect luncheon choice on a warm summer day after a hike along the highway.

Serves 4

Amount — Ingredients

Amount	Ingredients
16 to 20 stalks	fresh, tender asparagus, tough ends broken off
1 Tablespoon	extra-virgin olive oil
1/2 teaspoon	kosher salt
20 sprigs	fresh thyme
4 slices	white, whole wheat or sourdough bread
1 clove	garlic, peeled
1 pinch	kosher salt
4 extra-large	eggs
5 ounces	Fontina or Gruyère cheese, sliced into 4 slices, 1/8-inch thick
2 ounces	prosciutto or Serrano ham, thinly sliced into about 8 slices
	extra virgin olive oil for drizzling over the sandwiches
	freshly cracked black pepper, to taste.

Instructions

To roast the asparagus: Adjust the oven rack to the middle position and preheat to 450° F. To check the asparagus for tenderness before roasting, bite into the end. If it's stringy and tough, peel off the outer layer at the bottom inch or two of each stalk.

Place the asparagus in a large bowl, drizzle the olive oil over it and sprinkle it with salt, tossing to coat. Scatter the thyme sprigs onto a baking sheet and lay the asparagus stalks over them. Roast in the oven for about 10 minutes, until tender to the touch yet firm in the center.

In a medium saucepan, start 2 quarts of water toward a boil for poaching the eggs.

Next, rub one side of each slice of bread with the garlic clove and place on a baking sheet, garlic side up. Layer with prosciutto, then asparagus and cheese. Adjust the oven rack to the upper position, and preheat the broiler. Heat under broiler until cheese melts, being careful not to burn it.

Meanwhile, poach the eggs in the saucepan with boiling water.

To poach the eggs: Crack an egg into a small bowl to check that the yolk is not broken. Slowly stir the water in one direction to create a whirlpool effect. Once the whirlpool has slowed a little, carefully slide the egg into the water against the side of the pan, following the water current as you pour it in so that the white envelops the yolk. Crack another egg into the small bowl and add to the water in the same manner. Poach the eggs for 2 to 2-1/2 minutes, until the whites are set and the yolks are runny. Remove bread from broiler. Carefully place the poached egg on top of the prosciutto, asparagus and cheese.

Drizzle sandwich with olive oil and freshly cracked pepper.

MR. CHRISTMAS

For those of us who have Christmas running through our veins, the taste of warm, spicy gingerbread, the notes of "Silent Night" and the smell of fresh pine boughs transport us to our favorite time of year – no matter if it's July and seagulls are floating gracefully over the shore.

One hot July day, we scrambled through the woods and over the rocky shore to Fall River, one of our favorite swimming holes. Picnic basket in tow, we came upon a beautiful red wooden canoe floating lazily in the river, a white sail fluttering in the breeze. There on the beach in front a campfire, amidst wood chips and birch bark, sat a bearded stranger.

Not wanting to disturb his solitude, we asked if he'd mind us having a picnic and a swim a little farther down the shore.

"OK by me," he assured us with a good-natured smile.

After a few delicious hours of swimming and soaking in the hot afternoon sun, we packed our picnic basket, now empty, and tramped back the way we had come. We stopped to thank this modern-day voyageur for sharing the Lake Superior shore with us.

Soon, though, we were engrossed in conversation about all manner of things … his love for the North Shore and a trip he made around Lake Superior, his 1940s vintage wooden canoe, the birch basket and canoe paddle he was making, and life in general. In those sunny, summer moments a friendship was carved, as surely as he carved the canoe paddle that lay on the rocks beside us. His presence that day became for us one of life's unexpected gifts.

A few days later, Steve Wingard walked the mile or so to The Pie Place for lunch. It was good to see him again, and we picked up our conversation as if no time or space passed since our day on the shore.

Mr. Christmas continues his Lake Superior voyage. (photo courtesy Steve Wingard)

As he sat at the table eating his sandwich, a little boy of 3 or 4 came in with his parents. In the innocent and exuberant fashion of the very young, his dark eyes took in the bearded man across the room. With a face full of excitement and belief, the little boy opened his arms wide and ran over to Steve's table.

"Hi, Christmas!" he cried in eager greeting.

Mr. Christmas, a twinkle in his own eyes, look fondly back at him.

This little boy had found the wonder of Christmas.

It hardly mattered that it was July.

Ice House Stack

Paddling a canoe takes a lot of energy, but this sandwich made Steve smack his lips with pleasure and prepared him for the next leg of his canoe journey. Though caramelizing the onions may take a little extra time, the rich, robust flavor is well worth it. If you can't find Gruyere, a nice Swiss cheese works just as well.

Serves 4

Amount / Ingredients

Amount	Ingredients
12 ounces	sliced roast beef
6 ounces	Gruyère cheese, sliced
4	soft buns

Horseradish Sauce

2/3 cup	Hellmann's mayonnaise
4 Tablespoons	prepared horseradish

Caramelized Onions

2 large	onions, sliced
1 Tablespoon	butter or olive oil
1/3 teaspoon	salt
1/3 teaspoon	sugar
1 Tablespoon	balsamic vinegar or red wine

Instructions

Caramelize onions first. Start by putting 1 tablespoon of butter or oil in a heavy skillet and heat on medium-high heat. When oil sizzles, add onions and spread evenly across the pan. Do NOT stir.

After 10 minutes, sprinkle with salt and sugar. Then you may stir and reduce heat to low. It is important not to stir too frequently. Only stir as you see the bottom layer of onions browning. Do not allow the onions to burn. Continue process 30 minutes to 1 hour, until caramelizing is complete. You may want to deglaze the pan with 1 tablespoon of balsamic vinegar or some red wine, to loosen sugars attached to the pan. (Any onion you do not use for sandwiches is great for other purposes, like adding to green beans, quiches, etc.)

To assemble sandwich, spread horseradish-mayonnaise mixture over both sides of a soft bun. Cover one side with 3 ounces of sliced roast beef, a satisfying layer of caramelized onion and a layer of Gruyere cheese. Place open face under a broiler until cheese has melted. Top with bun and serve.

Recipe Notes

Recipe Notes

Main Dishes & Memories

THE FISH THAT DIDN'T GET AWAY

One of many fish that didn't get away from Don.
(photo by Ted Weinberg)

There's a bit of Hemingway in him – his passion for fishing, his love for spinning a yarn, his bearded face and twinkling eyes.

Don Larmouth and his wife, Judy, have been our customers and treasured friends for many years. A storyteller extraordinaire, his fish tales always seem to have a happy ending. Whether it's tarpon fishing in the warm turquoise waters of the Florida Keys or fly fishing in the icy green waters of Ireland, Don always seems to net his catch.

An avid fisherman since childhood, Don has a comprehensive knowledge of fishing. The book and articles he has written attest to this.

One day, after breakfast at The Pie Place and after many questions from Josh, our chef who had just gotten his first fly-fishing rod, Don walked back to his cabin, a rustic, hand-hewn beauty, and wrote an inventory of pointers to assist the budding fly-fisherman. In Don, who has a passion for teaching and fishing, the professor and fisherman merge triumphant.

Josh has spent many hours wading the rivers and floating the inland lakes with Don, learning the art of fly fishing. From tying the most exquisite flies – I call them pretty, much to Don's consternation – to netting incredibly beautiful fish, Don expresses the art of man in nature.

As most fly fishermen espouse, Don is a catch-and-release kind of guy. However, on a rare occasion, he allows himself the opportunity to relish the culinary reward of his craft.

One day, he strode into our kitchen, creel over his shoulder, to present us with a magnificent brook trout.

"I'd like you to prepare it for Judy and me for dinner tonight," he said. "Prepare it however you like, but leave the head on and present it in its entirety."

We pondered the perfect way to prepare this fish, now a sacred task and one not taken lightly. We stuffed the cavity with thin slices of lemon and bunches of fresh thyme from our garden. We brushed the rosy, iridescent flesh with clarified butter, wrapping it in foil and placing it gently on the grill.

Served on a bed of wild rice pilaf and garnished with thyme sprigs, we carried it in procession to Don and Judy's table. Handing him a knife, and standing aside in anticipation, we watched as he cut into the fish, uncovering the succulent goodness nestled beneath the skin. He sampled the first bite like a sommelier tasting that first musky swallow of wine and nodded.

"Perfect," he declared. For the first time in Pie Place history, we shared in the feast, and it was good.

Don's passion for fishing and for teaching others to fish always brings to mind a quote from Ernest Hemingway. "The most solid advice for a writer is this, I think: Try to learn to breathe deeply, really to taste food when you eat, and when you sleep, really sleep. Try as much as possible to be wholly alive with all your might, and when you laugh, laugh like hell. Try to be alive!"

Fresh Grilled Trout with Lemon, Fresh Thyme & Butter

This is a meal that Ernest Hemingway would relish with gusto. Our friend Don brought in a brook trout, but you can grill whatever fresh trout you're lucky enough to reel in. Rainbow or lake trout would be great, just keep in mind that lake trout will taste a bit fishy due to that excess fat necessary to keep Lake Superior fish warm. For a nice presentation, be brave and plate the trout leaving the head and tail intact. Or nestle the fish on a bed of fragrant thyme, tucking in thin slices of lemon. This meal will create quite a splash!

Makes 2 to 3 servings

Amount   Ingredients

Amount	Ingredients
1	trout, cleaned, may use fillets
4 to 6 Tablespoons	butter, cut into pats
2 to 3	lemons, sliced
3 bunches	fresh thyme leaves

Instructions

If using a gas or charcoal grill, preheat to 400° F.

Rinse the trout and pat it dry. If you have the whole fish, stuff the cleaned cavity with butter, lemon slices, and fresh thyme (quantity depends on the size of the fish). Wrap in foil and place on the grill. If you are using fillets, place butter, lemon and thyme in foil. Cook approximately 15 to 20 minutes, turning frequently. Unwrap foil to check fish and serve when the flesh is firm and white. You may need more time, if it is a larger trout.

THOSE JORDAN GIRLS &
OTHER STORIES OF LIFE

Literature may be the poetic memory of Humanity.
– Elie Wiesel

We are a family that loves to read. Voracious in our appetite, we devour books as a child eats a peanut butter sandwich – with enthusiasm for each and every morsel.

Many Pie Place guests and friends share our passion for reading. In the café, mealtimes often are spiced with animated conversations about a good book that they, or we, are reading. It's a treat to share the adventure of a story with someone as impassioned about it as you.

Over the years, we've received platesful of good reads from customers, introducing us to new authors and subjects that we might not have stumbled upon without their urgings.

One wise and wonderful woman, with dancing eyes and a passion for reading, brought a list of five book titles and authors unknown to me. I proceeded to make my way through each and every one – a feast for my soul. Now each time Joan Drury comes for a meal at The Pie Place, we eagerly exchange our newest must-read list of freshly found stories and authors.

Sometimes I get to pass the platter of good reading from one guest to another. When some guests recommended Richard Powers' *The Time of Our Singing*, the lyricism of his 1939 love story and marriage of a Jewish scientist and African-American singer moved me to the depths of my being. I recommended it to Joan, and we experienced the intimacy of a great book shared. Forming our own

Joan and Gertie in a comfortable reading chair. (photo by Ellen Stubbs)

Drury Lane Bookstore sits not far from Lake Superior. (photo by Mary Beams)

"book club of two," we discussed how this book's perspective on relationships and differences caused us to look at our own world in a new way. Both of us had the same experience of pausing after reading a few pages to process the nuances and profound meanings. It was a thrill to examine one of my favorite books with a person I hold dear personally and in high esteem "literarily."

Joan knows how to judge a book. She is a writer, a published author in fact, and the owner of our favorite local bookstore, Drury Lane Books. Not only has Joan recommended to me what became some of my favorite books, she's written one. *Those Jordan Girls* is the story of a family of women, strong in their opinions and love for each other. It is set during the tumultuous civil rights movement. I adored it.

I remember finishing her book on my birthday. Sitting on a rocky ledge overlooking Lake Superior, a sumptuous gourmet picnic beside me and wrapped in a warm woolen blanket, I finished the final pages. It was a perfectly wondrous birthday gift – a story about women and choices (the ones we must choose to be true to ourselves) and how, in the end, it's love that pulls all the tangled edges back together and gives our life substance and meaning.

I walked through the woods, savoring those last words of the book, knowing Joan in a deeper, more intimate way and knowing myself a little better, too.

Words can be like comfort food. They feed us, they nurture us and they connect us. Virginia Woolf once said, "One cannot think well, love well, sleep well, if one has not dined well."

When I returned home that day, I called Joan to thank her.

I dined on more than food that day.

Shaker Chicken & Biscuits

Just as Joan loves good literature, she also enjoys "comfort food" that sustains and nurtures. Creamy and rich Shaker chicken and biscuits, flaky chicken pot pie or warm maple pecan pie – this is soul food that conjures family and friends. This recipe brings a divine complement of tender chicken and a luscious buttery gravy and can be served over warm, flaky biscuits or fluffy mashed potatoes. As Joan so aptly termed it, "It's not only delicious, but has a soft pleasing texture." This time-honored Shaker recipe is reminiscent of a simpler way of life and of taking the time to slow down for a good meal.

Serves 6

Amount — Ingredients

Amount	Ingredients
1 whole (3 pounds)	chicken, quartered
6 cups	water
1 teaspoon	salt
1/2 teaspoon	pepper
1 Tablespoon	chicken fat (from the reduced stock in kettle)
4 Tablespoons	butter
4 Tablespoons	flour
1 cup	heavy cream

Cream Biscuits

Makes 12 to 16

Amount	Ingredients
2 cups	bread flour, sifted
3 teaspoons	baking powder
1 cup	heavy cream

Instructions

Put chicken in large kettle, cover with water and season with salt and pepper. Cook uncovered for about an hour. When tender and the water is nearly boiled out (about 2 inches remaining), remove pieces, discard skin and bones and reserve liquid.

Use 1 tablespoon of the chicken fat from the reduced stock, add to it the butter and flour, whisking constantly, cook 2 minutes.

Add 2 cups chicken liquid, also from the reduced stock, and cream. Cook until gravy is thick and smooth. When adding salt to taste be very careful; it will go from too little salt to too much in an instant.

To prepare the cream biscuits: Preheat oven to 450° F. Sift flour and baking powder together. Whip cream until stiff. Mix lightly with flour, using fork. Turn onto lightly floured board and knead for 1 minute. Pat dough to 1/2 inch thickness and cut with biscuit cutter. Bake for 12 minutes or until golden brown.

Split and butter biscuits and lay on a platter. Pull the chicken into pieces and lay the chicken on the biscuits. Pour the gravy over the chicken and biscuits and serve. If you want to plate each serving separately, this works, too. Do whatever best pleases your family.

"It was a perfectly wondrous birthday gift — a story about . . . and how, in the end, it's love that pulls all the tangled edges back together."

HARVEY

A strapping Harvey and his team logging for Hedstrom's Lumber Company. (photo from Harvey Anderson collection)

Our friend Harvey Anderson, an "old Swede" as he calls himself, is as exuberant and full of life at 91 as he was as a strapping 25-year-old teamster.

In those early days, Harvey drove a team of draft horses that pulled felled logs from the Minnesota forests. The work was hard, and he loved it. Harvey enjoyed the solitude of the forest and of working with his team of horses.

Harvey has pictures of those days that show a jaunty young man clad in a plaid flannel shirt, a leather harness thrown over his shoulder.

Today, some 60 years later, Harvey still chops his own firewood. He plants and tends a large garden. He supplies his many friends and neighbors with fresh produce: vine-ripened tomatoes, beans, carrots, beets and his "Swede's favorites" – potatoes and rutabagas.

Often, these gifts of nature's bounty and Harvey's hands become a rich and savory stew. As the flavors of garden vegetables marry in the pot, the aroma of friendship and love waft through the kitchen. In the true Swedish tradition that tells us what is mine belongs to you, too, we dine together.

What a legacy. What a gift.

Beer Beef Stew

This classic stew, simmered with beer and a marriage of earthy flavors can be enhanced with your own garden vegetables or those of a gardening friend. As Harvey might say without pomp: "Real good!"

Serves 6

Amount — Ingredients

Amount	Ingredients
1/4 to 1/2 cup	flour
1/4 teaspoon	salt
1 teaspoon	freshly ground pepper
3 pounds	lean beef stew meat, cut into 1-inch cubes, use chuck (our pick) or round
4 Tablespoons	vegetable oil
2	yellow onions, sliced and rings separated
6 cloves	garlic, minced
2 cups	beef stock or canned beef broth
1 cup	beer, allowed to go flat
1	bay leaf
1 Tablespoon	brown sugar
2 Tablespoons	red wine vinegar
1 Tablespoon	Dijon mustard
2 teaspoons	dried thyme
1/2 cup	fresh chopped parsley
2 teaspoons	salt
1/4 teaspoon	freshly ground pepper
6 to 8	russet potatoes, peeled and cut into medium chunks
6	carrots, peeled and cut into medium chunks
8 ounces	fresh mushrooms, sliced
1 large	onion (very coarsely diced) or 6 ounces of pearl onions
	cornstarch, for thickening

Instructions

Preheat oven to 350° F. On a sheet of waxed paper, combine flour, salt and pepper. Toss meat in mixture to coat.

In a soup pot over medium-high heat, warm 2 tablespoons oil. Brown meat in batches, adding more oil if needed, about 10 minutes. With a slotted spoon remove meat to a plate. Add 1 tablespoon oil to pot and sauté onion and garlic until soft, about 5 minutes.

Add stock and beer and deglaze pan, stirring with a wooden spoon to loosen browned bits.

Add remaining ingredients except for vegetables, return meat to broth and bring to a boil. Reduce heat and simmer 1-1/2 hours. Peel vegetables and cut into medium chunks. Once meat is tender, add vegetables and simmer and additional 20 to 30 minutes. Remove bay leaf. Thicken if necessary with cornstarch and water.

THE DANCER

A portrait of Millie dressed for pow wow dancing. (photo courtesy Swartz family)

Her children brought her to dinner on Mother's Day. Layers of soft pink chiffon flowed over a tall, strong woman's body, and I was touched by the tennis shoes peeking from beneath her dress.

"You look beautiful," I said. "We are so glad you could come."

Millie Longbody Swartz smiled, openly pleased, a face tempered early from hardship, yet shy at the attention. She dined like a queen, savoring every bite and exclaiming with joy about the nuances of flavor. Oh, what a gift it was to serve her.

She thanked us with such graciousness and warmth, and it was one of those times that if we had served no one else that day, this would have been enough.

I was struck again by her feet as she left. Though hidden in tennis shoes, they seemed young feet, full-of-life feet.

I later learned that she leads the dancers in the Grand Entry at the Grand Portage pow wow. I could imagine her body releasing itself to the rhythm of the drums. Her beaded moccasins pounding the earth, twirling, swirling, doeskin clinging to strong thighs, feathers … flying!

Waussae/ aukonae k'weeyou; bright with flame is your body. – from Ojibway Ceremonies by Basil Johnston

Make-Ahead Crêpes

Millie enjoyed crêpes on Mother's Day, but they don't need to be a rare treat and can be served any time by making this basic crêpe recipe ahead and filling it later.

Makes 24 crêpes

Amount	Ingredients
2 cups	all-purpose flour
1/2 teaspoon	salt
2 cups	whole milk
1 cup	water
1 Tablespoon	butter, melted, plus some for coating the pan
4 large	eggs

102

Instructions

Combine flour and salt in a medium bowl. Place milk, water, butter and eggs in a blender; process until combined. Add flour mixture to blender; process until smooth. Cover and refrigerate for 1 hour.

Heat a 10-inch crêpe pan or nonstick skillet over medium-high heat. Coat pan lightly with butter. Remove pan from heat. Pour a scant 1/4 cup batter into pan, quickly tilting in all directions so batter covers the pan with a thin film. Cooks in about 1 minute. Carefully lift edge of crêpe with spatula to test for doneness. The crêpe is ready to turn when it can be easily loosened from the pan and is lightly brown. Turn it over and cook for 30 seconds on other side.

Place crêpe on a paper towel; cool completely. Repeat procedure, stirring batter between crêpes. Stack crêpes between single layers of wax paper or paper towels to prevent sticking. Store in plastic bag or large storage container. Can be refrigerated up to five days or frozen for up to two months.

Creamy Chicken Mushroom Crêpes

Serves 12

Amount / Ingredients

Amount	Ingredients
1 slice	applewood-smoked bacon, diced
1 pound	skinless, boneless chicken breast, cut into 1/2-inch pieces
1/4 cup	minced shallots (about 2)
1 teaspoon	chopped fresh thyme
1 package (8-ounce size)	pre-sliced mushrooms
1-1/4 cups	whole milk
1-1/2 Tablespoons	all-purpose flour
1/2 cup	shredded Gruyère cheese (4 ounces)
2 Tablespoons	chopped fresh parsley
1/2 teaspoon	salt
1/4 teaspoon	freshly ground pepper
12	Make-Ahead Crêpes

Instructions

Cook bacon in a large nonstick skillet over medium-high heat until crisp. Remove bacon, but leave the drippings in the pan; set bacon aside. Add chicken to drippings to flavor and sauté 3 minutes or until browned. Add shallots, thyme, mushrooms; sauté 5 minutes or until tender.

Combine milk and flour in a bowl, whisking until well blended. Gradually stir this mixture into chicken mixture; bring to a boil. Reduce heat and simmer until thick (about 2 minutes). Remove from heat; stir in bacon, cheese, parsley, salt and pepper. Spoon about 1/4 cup chicken mixture in center of each crêpe and roll up. Use a drizzle of the mixture as a sauce on top. You can prepare and refrigerate the chicken filling up to one day ahead. Reheat in a large non-stick skillet over medium heat for about 10 minutes. Reheat the crêpes in a warm pan or use a griddle flipping once.

THE PRAYER

*"Let this be our prayer
When we lose our way,
Lead us to a place
Guide us with your grace,
To a place where we'll be safe."*

The rich melodious strains of Andrea Bocelli waft and mingle with the fragrance of food from the kitchen. As I approach the table, our guest has tears running down his cheeks.

"Are you OK, sir?" I asked as I refill his water glass.

"Who is singing this beautiful music?" inquired this big, burly man of a man.

"Andrea Bocelli, he's an Italian opera singer."

"I've never been much for opera," he said, "but this guy really moves me."

After dinner, as he was about to drive away, I ran to the car and handed him the tape. "I think you should have this," I said, and he drove away as tears came to his eyes once more.

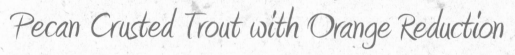

A big-hearted man and his family - Bruce, Nancy, and Alex. (photo by Chris Ellickson)

So began our friendship with Bruce, Nancy and Alex. Bruce and his family, avid anglers and lovers of the North Shore, became Pie Place regulars, coming to eat and spin their fish stories.

One hectic summer day, Bruce and his fishing compadres poked their heads through the back door. "Come on out here," said Bruce with his big bear-hug smile. "There's something I want to show you."

There, gleaming in the sun, were 30 pounds of fresh-caught lake trout. "Thought these might work for dinner tonight."

Suffice it to say that our customers dined happily that night on the freshest, most succulent fish in town. We gave thanks for the gift of fresh fish, and for the gift of Bruce, his family and their generosity.

Pecan Crusted Trout with Orange Reduction

This is a great way to prepare that fresh trout pulled out of the lake this morning. If your fish got away, or you're not on the North Shore, you can purchase fresh fish from your local fish market or grocery store. Either way, you'll love this recipe. Bruce always gives his compliments to the chef.

Serves 4

Amount	Ingredients
2 cups	pecans
1 cup	all-purpose flour
2 large	trout, filleted without skin
	salt and pepper
3 large	egg whites, whisked lightly to mix

Orange Reduction Sauce

Amount	Ingredients
1-1/2 cups	orange juice
1 cup	dry white wine
2/3 cup	chopped shallots
1/4 cup	white wine vinegar
8 stems	parsley, about 5-inch long stems
1 sprig	thyme
1-1/2 Tablespoons	lemon juice
2 sprigs	fresh rosemary
1/4 cup	heavy cream
3/4 cup	unsalted butter, cut into 12 pieces

Sauteed Vegetables

Amount	Ingredients
3 Tablespoons	olive oil, divided
1	carrot, peeled, cut into matchsticks
1	red bell pepper, thinly sliced
6 cups	Savoy cabbage, thinly sliced
2 Tablespoons	unsalted butter
	fresh chives, chopped, for garnish

Instructions

Combine pecans and 1 tablespoon of flour in food processor. Grind pecans finely, transfer to plate. Place remaining flour on another plate. Sprinkle fish with salt and pepper. Dip fillets in flour to coat, shake off excess. Using pastry brush, brush one side with egg whites. Press egg-white side onto pecans to coat with nuts. Transfer to waxed paper-lined baking sheet, pecan side down. Chill.

To prepare sauce: Combine orange juice, white wine, shallots, vinegar, parsley stems, thyme and lemon juice in saucepan. Boil 10 minutes, add rosemary. Boil until reduced to 1/2 cup, about 10 minutes. Strain into another saucepan. Add cream, bring to a gentle boil. Reduce heat to medium-low. Whisk in butter, 1 piece at a time (do not boil). Season with salt and pepper.

Heat 2 tablespoons oil in a heavy large pan over high heat. Add carrot and bell pepper, toss 2 minutes. Add cabbage, toss until it wilts, about 4 minutes. Salt and pepper it. Remove from heat.

Melt 2 tablespoons butter with 1 tablespoon olive oil in heavy large skillet over medium-high heat. Place 2 fillets, pecan side down, into skillet. Cook until crust is gold and crisp, about 2 minutes. Using spatula, turn fillets over. Cook until just opaque in center, about 2 minutes. Transfer to plate. Whisk sauce over low heat until warm. Divide vegetables among plates. Top with trout fillets and spoon sauce over fish and vegetables. Garnish with chopped chives and serve.

Because She Asked Me To

They have been a part of The Pie Place family for so long; I can't seem to pull from my memory the first time Ted and Eileen Weinberg came into the restaurant.

It's like that sometimes. People's lives become intertwined with yours so that you truly can't remember life without them.

We await their arrival, catching up on the local happenings in their absence and poring over pictures of the newest grandchild.

"They're breeding like rabbits!" Ted exclaims playfully, a proud grandfather. Imagine going from the first grandchild to a gaggle of 11 in a mere four years. Ted and Eileen are doting grandparents, savoring each new arrival and passing on stories of the evolution of this close-knit family.

But this story begins 46 years ago, when Ted began courting Eileen, a beautiful young woman from Chicago. Smitten and wanting to show her the Boundary Waters that he loved, Ted took her on a canoe trip. Ted had met and become friends with Dorothy Molter, the legendary "Root Beer Lady," during his early paddling trips, and he wanted the two of them to meet. Though a city girl, Eileen fell in love with the pristine rivers and majestic pines. She felt an immediate kindred connection with Dorothy and her North Woods home and vowed then and there that someday she and Ted would have a home here, too.

"Eileen is the glue that has held our family together," says Ted with immense love and pride. True

Eileen and Ted Weinberg in a photo by daughter Rachel.

Eileen and Ted with Dorothy Molter between them.

106

Eileen and Ted with the grandchildren for a family portrait by the Big Lake. (photos courtesy of the Weinberg family)

to her commitment and their shared dream, they bought a quaint stone cottage nestled beside a river on the shores of Lake Superior.

They restored it with loving care and an eye for detail and created a home for their children, grandchildren and many friends. It is a place imbued with the essence of the North Woods, a place where memories are made.

Ted loves our Beef Stout Pie and calls ahead frequently to have us make one to serve to close friends or family.

It's a culinary event when we carry one, fresh and flaky from the oven, to his table, the ale-scented aroma filling the restaurant. Ted sniffs the pie like a connoisseur taking in the bouquet of a fine wine and pronounces it good.

Every time Ted raves about it and, every time, extra care goes into making it. Cooking is much like performing in a play; you say the same lines every night, but you strive to infuse them with as much passion each night as if it were opening night.

Ted came into the restaurant one spring day to grab a bowl of soup on his way to their cabin. An avid fly fisherman, Ted finds that nothing can soothe life's hectic pace quite like a few quiet hours on the river.

He told me about an upcoming marathon he was planning to run with his daughter Rachel, who lives in Chicago.

"I didn't know you were a runner," I said, surprised he had never mentioned it before.

"I'm not," he said.

I laughed incredulously, envisioning what it would mean for him to prepare for such an event. "Then why are you doing it?"

"Because she asked me to."

For a loving father – enough said.

Beef Stout Pie

Savory meat pies are an essential of good country cooking. Served right from the oven, the flaky crust, tender chunks of beef, and mushrooms create a truly festive meal. To Ted, it's worth a phone call to make sure it's there.

Serves 4 to 6

Amount — Ingredients

Amount	Ingredients
4 Tablespoons	flour, divided, plus extra for dusting
1/2 teaspoon	mustard powder, we prefer Colman's English mustard powder
	salt and pepper
1-1/2 pounds	sirloin steak, cut in 1/2-inch cubes
1/4 cup	olive oil
3/4 cup	pearl onions, peeled or the frozen kind are already peeled
	or 1 small onion, chopped
1 package (8-ounce size)	fresh white mushrooms, sliced
1 bottle	stout or dark beer, divided, we like Guinness best
3 cans (14-ounce size)	beef consommé
4 sprigs	fresh thyme leaves
2 Tablespoons	Worcestershire sauce
1 recipe (pg. 129)	crust round, 12-inch
1	egg white, beaten
2 Tablespoons	half-and-half, for glazing the crust
1/4 cup	water, for the roux

Instructions

Mix 2 tablespoons of flour, mustard powder and salt and freshly ground pepper in a large bowl. Add the meat and toss to coat it well with the seasoned flour. Heat the oil (add a little butter with the oil if you like) in a soup pot over high heat. Add the onions and brown them lightly, 3 to 4 minutes. Using a slotted spoon, remove the onions and set aside. Sauté the sliced mushrooms until golden and set aside.

Add the cubes of meat to the pot, in batches, if necessary, and brown them on all sides. Add onions and mushrooms to meat.

Stir in the stout, 2 cans consommé, thyme and Worcestershire sauce. Bring to a boil, then lower the heat, cover, and simmer for 1-1/ 2 hours. Stir in the reserved onions, remove the thyme, and simmer until the meat is tender, about 30 minutes more. If the mixture seems thin, you can add a roux. Create a roux by whisking 2 tablespoons of flour with 1/4 cup of water until smooth. Reserve the remaining roux for the gravy.

Preheat the oven to 375° F.

On a floured surface, roll out the pastry dough to a 11- to 12-inch round, large enough to cover the pie generously. Lay the dough evenly in a deep dish pie pan or tin. Ladle the cooked filling into the pastry, distributing it evenly. Fold the excess dough up to cover the mixture, gently "pleating" as necessary. This creates a rustic, yet elegant, crust reminiscent of a country-style galette or tart. Brush the crust with a mixture of beaten egg white and half-and-half to glaze. Place in 375° oven and bake for 45 to 50 minutes, until the crust is golden brown and flaky.

For the gravy: Put 1 can beef consommé in a pan. Add a few sprigs of thyme plus 1/8 cup beer. Bring to a boil, reduce to simmer, and thicken with roux. Present on the side in a gravy boat for those who like to add gravy.

THE BIRD SEED ANGELS

We are avid "kitchen birders," watching the birds that frequent the feeder hanging from a branch outside our kitchen window.

Our bird list grows every year, as our feathered friends have come to know The Pie Place as "the" place to eat.

Blue jays, hummingbirds, pine grosbeaks, redpolls, cedar waxwings, woodpeckers, nuthatches and our beloved chickadees keep us company and give us hours of enjoyment.

Buddy fills our birdfeeders every day. He has an important role in keeping our birds fat and sassy. He talks to them as he feeds them, and they have come to know and trust him.

The deer also frequent the feeder. They stroll in at night, necks craned, soft noses pointed to the heavens as they use their long, wet tongues

Denny & Lucy and birdseed in bloom.
(photo by Denny Fitzpatrick)

to reach the seeds, devouring their fill. Their dining etiquette, not as refined as the birds, wreaked havoc with the feeder. Eager teeth chewed the wood and left it hanging haphazardly from its branch.

One thing we know for sure – angels come in the quietude of the night.

One morning we came to the restaurant, focused on preparing for the day, when we looked out the window. There swinging happily in the breeze was a beautiful, very sturdy, birdfeeder. Brimming with sunflower seeds, it had already attracted a motley (or is it molt-ly?) crew of feathered friends. Fifty pounds of seed filled a shiny new garbage can, protecting it from our furry, four-legged customers, big and small.

"I know who brought all this," exclaimed Buddy, a mischievous grin on his face.

Buddy, his sister Maryl Skinner (aka Lucy), and brother-in-law Denny Fitzpatrick had come treading softly in the twilight hours … our birdseed angels.

The birds were so happy about their refined dining arrangements, they wrote a melodious thank you note to Buddy, Lucy and Denny. Being birds, they kept it simple: "Dear birdseed angels, we love you!"

Artichoke & Spring Vegetable Stew
with Sweet Potato Dumplings

Denny & Maryl prefer meatless dishes, and this spring vegetable stew is among their favorites.

Serves 6

Amount	Ingredients

Dumplings

Amount	Ingredients
1 medium	sweet potato (about 12 ounces), peeled and cut into large chunks
1-1/2 teaspoon	coarse salt
1-1/2 cups	all-purpose flour
1/2 teaspoon	baking powder
	freshly ground pepper
2 large	eggs, lightly beaten
2 Tablespoons	finely chopped fresh flat-leaf parsley

Stew

Amount	Ingredients
2	lemons, halved
4 medium	fresh artichokes (10 ounces each) or 2 cans (14-ounce size) artichoke hearts
3 Tablespoons	unsalted butter
10 ounces	pearl onions, blanched and peeled
1 rind	Parmesan cheese about 5 inches long; or substitute 5-inch piece cheese
2-1/2 cups	homemade or low-sodium store-bought vegetable stock (not roasted)
1 teaspoon	coarse salt, plus additional to taste
1/4 teaspoon	freshly ground pepper, plus additional to taste
12	orange or yellow carrots, peeled, halved lengthwise, cut into 3-inch pieces
2 Tablespoons	finely chopped fresh tarragon
6 ounces	asparagus, trimmed and cut into 3-inch pieces (about 1-1/4 cups)
4-1/2 cups	water

Instructions

Make the dumplings: Place sweet potato in a saucepan; cover with water by 1 inch. Bring to a boil; add a large pinch of salt. Reduce heat; simmer until tender, about 15 minutes. Meanwhile whisk the flour, baking powder, salt and a pinch of pepper in a bowl; set aside. Drain sweet potato. Spread out; let cool 15 minutes. Transfer to a bowl and mash with a fork or potato masher. Stir in eggs and parsley. Add flour mixture; stir just until a sticky dough forms.

Make stew: Squeeze juice of 1-1/2 lemons into water; add rinds. Remove and discard tough outer leaves from 1 artichoke. Cut off top third; peel stem. Halve artichoke lengthwise; remove fuzzy choke, and discard. Cut into 1-inch-thick wedges, and place in lemon water. Repeat with remaining artichokes. For those who don't want to take the time to use fresh artichokes, use canned artichokes. Melt butter in a medium stockpot over medium heat. Add onions, cook, stirring occasionally, 3 minutes. Add Parmesan rind. Drain artichokes; add to pot. Stir in stock and 4-1/2 cups water; add salt and pepper. Bring to a boil. Add carrots. Reduce heat; simmer, partially covered, 10 minutes. Squeeze remaining 1/2 lemon into pot; stir in tarragon.

Using 2 spoons, form 18 dumplings from the dough. Drop one at a time into stew as you work. Cover and cook 7 minutes without lifting the lid. Add asparagus. Cook, covered, until the dumplings are cooked through and vegetables are tender; another 3 minutes. Remove cheese rind before ladling into soup bowls.

The "Red Nose People"

What imaginary line does one cross when acquaintance turns into friendship, then friendship becomes family?

You walk across that boundary between heart beats; in a pulsing moment "hardly known" becomes "I can hardly remember life without you in it."

Pat and Katie Johnson and Paul and Pat West came into our life in much that way.

They came to the North Shore for a summer weekend, took a detour at the insistence of Patrick's Mom and appeared at The Pie Place for pie. We thoroughly enjoyed their company. Later that day, the gang showed up at Northern Impulses (our art gallery and gift store). We then began a conversation still going on 17 years later.

Kathy Rice joins Marie and Chris in adopting the Red Nose of honor. (photo by Patrick Johnson)

That evening, they reappeared at The Pie Place. Donning big bright red noses, they were seated ceremoniously amid stares (and smiles) from other guests. Jolly and mischievous to the core, they proceeded to gift us with our very own "noses."

"I will never put that thing on!" I insisted.

Suffice it to say, that by evening's end, we were all official members of the "Red Nose People" club – myself

included, clown nose and all. Now whenever a couple appears at The Pie Place wearing red noses, it's pretty obvious who recommended our restaurant.

Pat and Katie, Paul and Pat have been another unexpected gift. As Patrick is often heard to say (from under his red nose), "Enjoy every precious moment." And with them, we do.

Apple Cider Buttermilk Chicken

With all the flavors of late fall, this dish is requested again and again. It's a way to enjoy the tastes – as well as the colors – of the season. This luscious gravy must be ladled over fluffy mashed potatoes. We prepare this dish for Pat, Katie and friends whenever they come for a visit.

Serves 4 to 6

Amount   Ingredients

Amount	Ingredients
4 to 6	skinless, boneless packaged chicken breasts
1 cup	buttermilk
1 Tablespoon	butter
1	Granny Smith apple, cored, cut into 8 wedges, keep peel on
1	Red Delicious apple, cored, cut into 8 wedges, keep peel on
1 cup	apple cider
1 cup	canned chicken broth
1 cup	heavy cream
1 cup	flour
	salt and pepper, to taste

Instructions

Place chicken in single layer in a glass baking dish. Pour buttermilk over. Turn chicken to coat, cover and marinate overnight.

Melt butter in a heavy skillet over medium-high heat. Add apples, sauté until golden, about 5 minutes. Transfer apples to bowl. Add cider to the same skillet. Boil until cider is reduced to 1/2 cup, about 8 to 10 minutes. Add broth and cream. Boil until liquid is reduced to sauce consistency, about 15 minutes.

Drain chicken. Place flour in bowl. Season flour generously with salt and pepper. Coat chicken with flour. Heat butter in another heavy large skillet over medium heat. Add chicken and sauté until brown and cooked through, about 5 minutes per side. Transfer to plates, keep warm. Add sauce to skillet, scraping chicken bits with a wooden spoon. Return chicken breasts to sauce. Cover and simmer on stove for 1/2 hour. Season to taste with salt and pepper. When serving, drizzle chicken with sauce. Garnish with cooked apple slices, re-warmed quickly in the pan before topping the dish.

MEMORIES

We come to know our customers' favorite things, old-fashioned pumpkin pie, warm and grainy wild rice bread, or a steamy, herb-infused pot pie.

Rick Novitsky of Grand Portage loves simple food that nurtures the soul and piques memories of family and home. He draws friends around him like a warm woolen blanket and marvels at his world and the people in it.

One winter evening, Rick and his wife, Rosie, came in for dinner. While clearing the dishes from their table, I noticed a small, sleek object in his hand. "What's that?"

Rick snaps a photo of himself, Rosie and granddaughter Shaelynn.

Rick smiled broadly as he opened the box. A video danced on a tiny screen – images of his son and granddaughter overlaid by a tender song. Rick's obvious joy at creating this moment-in-time memory moved me beyond words. Peeking into his heart, I was seeing, through his eyes, those he holds dear.

"It's how I express what I feel," he said. "They're going through some tough times right now, and it's how I can deal with all the feelings inside of me. I've done others like this, one for Rosie. The words to a song stir me, have meaning for me, and I put them together with photographs and create memories."

How little we know of another until providence touches us and our inner selves are revealed.

We as a family share much in common with this gentle man, a love of music ("Sweet Baby James") and a love of carefully chosen words that bring us to a new understanding of who we are and how we relate to our world. Kindredship is born of this commonality, this shared love of song, and as James Taylor's words play through my head, I know that it is true:

"We are bound together, all men and women, living on the earth.
Ties of hope and love, sisters and brothers."

Voyageur Roasted Pork Loin with Apple Cider Glaze

We love pork, and combining it with fall apples and fresh-pressed cider, make this a perfect cold weather meal – and it is just the kind of meal that Rick and Rosie love. Though a bit more complex than most, this recipe is well worth the time and effort. We think it's hardy enough to fuel even the voyageurs!

Serves 8

Amount	Ingredients

Pork Loin

Amount	Ingredients
1/2 Tablespoon	mustard seeds
1 Tablespoon	peppercorns
2 Tablespoons	whole-grain mustard
1/4 cup	fresh chopped sage
1 5- to 6-pound	bone-in pork loin roast, or use boneless if you wish
1 Tablespoon	vegetable oil
1 Tablespoon	coarse salt

Cider Glaze

Amount	Ingredients
2	sweet-tart apples, we like Braeburns, but choose your favorite
1 small	sweet onion
2 cups	apple cider
1/4 cup	maple syrup
1 Tablespoon	prepared mustard, whole grain or Dijon are our preferred types
1/2 cup	packed brown sugar
1 Tablespoon	cider vinegar
1 pinch	ground clove

Instructions

Prepare the pork loin the day before. Crush the mustard seeds and peppercorns using a mortar and pestle. Blend into a paste with the mustard and sage. Rub the roast with vegetable oil and season it by rubbing all sides with the mustard paste. Cover the seasoned roast with plastic wrap and refrigerate overnight or for up to 24 hours.

Make the glaze the day of roasting. Core and slice the apples. Peel and thinly slice the onions. In a saucepan, whisk together the apple cider, maple syrup, mustard, brown sugar, cider vinegar, ground cloves, apple and onion slices. Heat over medium heat. Bring the mixture to a boil, reduce heat and simmer for 25 minutes until apples are cooked. Strain cooked mixture into a bowl by pressing through a sieve with a wooden spoon to extract all juices. Discard the solids.

To roast the pork: Position oven rack near the bottom of the oven and preheat to 420° F. Remove the seasoned roast from the refrigerator and allow it to sit at room temperature for about 1 hour. Sprinkle coarse salt over the roast. Place roast in oven and lower the heat to 325° F. Cook pork until internal temperature registers 130° on a meat thermometer, about 2 to 2-1/2 hours.

Raise oven temperature to 350° F and baste the roast with the cider glaze, every 10 minutes for 30 minutes. When the roast reaches 150 degrees internal temperature remove from the oven. Let roast rest on a cutting board for 20 minutes and then slice.

Add 1/4 cup water in the roasting pan and place the pan on the stove over medium-high heat, scraping the brown bits from the bottom with a wooden spoon. Whisk in any remaining cider glaze and blend it with the pan juices, skimming off fat if necessary. Simmer for 2 to 3 minutes to reduce the liquid and fully incorporate the rich flavors.

Present and carve the roast. Serve the roast with the pan juices in a gravy boat so that your guests can ladle it over the meat. Simple mashed potatoes make the best side.

Pay It Forward

He ambled into the restaurant one frosty fall day, rugged and handsome in a young man sort of way.

He smelled of wood smoke and of being a long time in the woods, eager to fill his belly with savory, warming soup. He'd been hiking and camping in the deep woods of the Gunflint Trail for a couple weeks, he explained, a much needed solitary retreat from the stress of college and the demands of those whose wishes were not his own.

Quietly he sat writing in a worn leather-bound journal, his demeanor sweet and appreciative as I placed the steaming bowl of soup before him.

He talked of running out of provisions two days before he was due to come out. Walking through the forest, hungry and ready to bed down for the night, he came upon a pair of hunters sitting in a clearing, having their supper beside a crackling fire. They invited him to share their food and sleep near the warmth of the campfire.

A painting of a grouse by our friend Mark Dunker.

Providence was surely looking down upon him that night.

While enjoying his soup, the young man and another guest struck up a conversation. After a long and animated visit, the gentleman bid his farewell. At the register, the man said in a whisper, "Put that young man's lunch on my bill."

When our young friend was rested and ready to leave, he asked for his bill. I told him the other man had paid.

He looked at me, incredulous. "I don't even know his name."

"It doesn't matter," I said. "You'll always remember his kindness and maybe some day, you can do the same for someone else."

"Would you mind coming outside?" he asked, a smile warming his wind-chapped face. "I have something for you." He opened a large worn canvas pack, gently taking out a ruffed grouse, its feathers russet and brown. Handing it to me, he said, "The hunters who shared their campsite with me last night gave this to me as I was leaving this morning. I'd like you to have it. Maybe you could have it for your dinner tonight."

I thanked him, wished him well, and he was on his way once again.

That night we feasted on roast grouse and wild lingonberry sauce. We didn't know his name, but it didn't matter. His gift would always be remembered … and we'll pass the generosity forward.

Ruffed Grouse with Lingonberry Sauce

Wild game is a part of our North Woods culture, and this simple meal lends itself to that tradition. If you don't have a hunter among your family or friends, or if wild grouse is not available, you can create a similar, quite elegant meal using Cornish game hens. Cooking time will be about the same. We think our young traveler would have been pleased with how we prepared his gift.

Serves 4

Amount — Ingredients

Amount	Ingredients
4	grouse, dressed
4 slices	bacon

Lingonberry Sauce

Amount	Ingredients
4 Tablespoons	butter, divided
1/2 cup	diced shallots
2/3 cup	dry white wine
3 Tablespoons	lingonberry jam

To Scandinavian immigrants, lingonberries are a taste of home.

Instructions

Preheat oven to 375° F.

Clean and rinse grouse; pat dry. Wrap one slice of bacon around each bird, tucking it under the bird. Place the birds in shallow pan and roast, uncovered in a 375° oven for about 1 hour or until no longer pink. Remove from oven and let rest for about 10 minutes. Remove bacon from each bird.

Sauce: Melt 2 tablespoons butter in a small saucepan over medium-high heat while grouse rests. Add shallots and sauté 5 minutes or until tender. Add wine; cook 10 minutes or until liquid is reduced by half. Reduce heat to low; whisk in lingonberry jam and remaining 2 tablespoons butter. Cook 2 minutes or until slightly thickened.

Drizzle lingonberry sauce over each grouse.

A special garnish, if you can get them, are fresh lingonberries. Used with fresh parsley, the two add a dash of color and texture. We are lucky; a dear friend brings us wild lingonberries from Saskatchewan every year. We use them in scones, sauces and a Christmastime jam – and, of course, as garnish.

ROCKIN'

Rocking … what image does that evoke in you? A wise old woman sitting on her porch, shucking peas and rocking peacefully back and forth? A boat rocking gently with the swell of the waves?

For Terry and Ila Martin, "rocking" means spending hours on the shores of Lake Superior gathering beautiful geologic specimens. They clamber over the craggy landscape like prospectors searching for elusive gold nuggets – but they prefer the perfect stone to place in their rock garden back home in Riverton, Minnesota.

Terry, Ila and Willow rockin' on the shore. (photo by Terry Martin)

Lovers of nature, they are happiest spending hours hiking, gathering rocks from the shore in summer, cross-country skiing in winter and soaking in the energy of the North Shore.

We came to know Terry and Ila several years ago, when they stopped by the restaurant for lunch. As so often happens, we hit it off right away, and The Pie Place became a destination for their frequent visits to Grand Marais. Though it seems we can feel them coming, they do try to sneak into town, surprising and delighting us with a visit.

Terry and Ila, retired but eternally young and full of life, find it easy to turn from their table to engage in a lively conversation with the guests at the table next to them.

One year they joined us for Thanksgiving. After enjoying a succulent traditional turkey dinner with all the trimmings, they left with appetites fulfilled and with newly found friends.

And another Pie Place tradition was established. The following year they returned at Thanksgiving again as did those friends. This time they sat together at the same table.

Terry loves to make things with his hands and fashions lamps from diamond willow. He also creates whimsical birdhouses with twisted vines, twigs, old tin scraps and weathered wood. He forages the forest and beaches for the perfect materials.

Terry made a birdhouse for us, presenting it with an elfish grin. Any bird would feel at home in it and we cherish it to this day – just as we do their presence in our life.

118

Turkey with Bramble Sauce

After a day spent gathering stones on their beloved Lake Superior shore, Terry and Ila enjoyed one of their favorite meals. Terry always asks for more sauce. Fresh fragrant herbs, plump blackberries and red currant jelly meld to create a vibrant sauce perfect for drizzling over roast turkey breast, pork tenderloin or roast chicken. Garnish with sprigs of fresh rosemary or thyme, for a truly sophisticated presentation.

Serves 4

Amount   Ingredients

Turkey

Amount	Ingredients
1 large	turkey breast, skin on
4 Tablespoons	dry white wine or hard cider
2 Tablespoons	chopped fresh rosemary
	pepper
	fresh rosemary sprigs and blackberries to garnish

Bramble Sauce

Amount	Ingredients
1-3/4 cups	blackberries
small bunch	fresh thyme leaves
4 Tablespoons	maple syrup
1 Tablespoon	apple cider
splash	white wine
2 Tablespoons	red currant jelly

Instructions

Preheat oven to 375° F.

Place turkey breast in a bowl. Sprinkle with the wine or hard cider and chopped rosemary and season to taste with pepper. Cover and set aside to marinate for at least an hour.

Drain the marinade and reserve for the sauce. Place breast skin side up on wire rack in broiler pan. Roast at 375° for approximately 1 hour, until meat is cooked and skin is golden.

To make the sauce, place the marinade in a pan with the blackberries and thyme, simmering gently until soft. Press through a strainer. Add maple syrup, apple cider, and a splash of white wine to the sauce.

Return the blackberry purée to the pan, add the red currant jelly, and bring to a boil. Reduce heat, stirring to combine the jelly, and gently simmer the sauce, uncovered, until it is reduced by about one-third. Pour into a gravy boat or drizzle slices of meat with the sauce.

Garnish with fresh rosemary or thyme sprigs and a few plump blackberries.

FROM GOOD STOCK

When I was young, I would go with Mother to our local butcher shop. Don stood behind a large wood chopping block, a white apron wrapped around his lean body. An enameled meat case with a curved-glass front displayed marbled cuts of red meat, chickens and farm fresh eggs, thick slabs of bacon and baskets of homemade sausage.

Every year at Christmastime, my mother asked Don to prepare a rolled roast – prime rib filled with herbs, spices, onions and garlic. I can still see it turning slowly on a rotisserie, burnished and glistening, as it perfumed our house on Christmas Eve. The best gravy Mom ever made came from meat juices that dripped into a roasting pan.

Great ingredients mean food served and memories made at the family table. Purveyors, those who supply food stuffs, are essential to a restaurateurs's success. Good purveyors provide the freshest herbs and salad greens, maple syrup, fresh-caught-fish, succulent sausages and cuts of meat.

At our local market, Johnson's Grocery, the butcher Marlo Larson is one of those purveyors without whom a successful restaurant cannot live. Who knew that in a village in a boreal forest

Marlo loves helping customers. (photo by Nadya Shkurdyuk)

120

nestled on the shores of Lake Superior, such a man in such a profession would exist?

True to his Norwegian heritage, Marlo is hard-working, open-hearted and eager to lend a hand. Marlo has used his Scandinavian ingenuity and creativity to expand his wares.

Charcuterie is a branch of cooking devoted to the preparation of foods such as bacon, ham, sausages, patés and confit, primarily from pork. Curing, brining, salting and smoking were among the early ways of preserving meat, before refrigeration was available. Just imagine the arduous task of cutting large blocks of ice from the frozen lake and hauling it by horse and sled to the icehouse to keep foods from spoiling. I read how the legendary Justine Kerfoot did just that at the Gunflint Lodge.

With almost daily regularity, I would call Marlo to say, "Hey Marlo (Minnesota speak), would you mind …?" No matter the request, his generous reply always is, "Why sure!" (also Minnesota speak). He happily debones, grinds, cubes or slices whatever we need for our weekly changing menu.

When we needed chorizo, Marlo made chorizo. If we wanted beef tenderloin, he'd order organic, grass-fed, cut to buttery perfection. Venison? Sure! Prosciutto? Yah sure! He even crafted a signature sausage for The Pie Place Café, something that our dear Cheryl dreamed about for years.

Marlo is following in the footsteps of a long line of butchers at Johnson's Grocery, starting here with one of the original Johnson brothers. (photo courtesy Robin Johnson)

I could go on and on (but I promised Marlo I wouldn't). Suffice it to say, Marlo has been a lifesaver more times than we can count. He provided us with quality meats, unsurpassed in this "grow 'em fast and get it to the table" day and age. Marlo saw our vision and helped us to make it a reality. A trusted friend, his generous spirit inspires all of us.

We love creating memories at The Pie Place, and good food helps to create them. Marlo has been a memory maker, too – from his hands, to our kitchen, to you at your table.

"Who knew that in a village in a boreal forest nestled on the shores of Lake Superior, such a man in such a profession would exist?"

Pasta with Pumpkin & Sausage

Marlo's homemade sausage adds pizzazz to this pasta. Crafted with care, this sweet sausage has a hint of piquant spicy flavor. We're lucky enough to have Marlo, but you can find a great local butcher and start your own flavor tradition, or find any sweet Italian sausage.

Serves 4

Amount — Ingredients

Amount	Ingredients
2 Tablespoons	extra virgin olive oil, divided
1 pound	bulk sweet Italian sausage
4 cloves	garlic, cracked and chopped
1 medium	onion, finely chopped
1	bay leaf, fresh or dried
4 to 6 sprigs	sage leaves, medium chopped (about 2 Tablespoons); or use about 1/2 Tablespoon of dried sage
1 cup	dry white wine
1 can (14-ounce size)	chicken stock
1 cup	canned pumpkin
1/2 cup	heavy cream
1/8 teaspoon	ground cinnamon
1/2 teaspoon	nutmeg, ground or freshly grated
	Coarse salt and black pepper
1 pound	penne rigate, cooked to al dente
	Romano or Parmigiano-Reggiano, for grating

Instructions

Heat a large, deep nonstick skillet over medium high heat. Add 1 tablespoon of olive oil to the pan and brown the sausage. Transfer sausage to paper towel lined plate. Drain fat from skillet and return pan to stove. Add the remaining tablespoon oil, and then the garlic and onion. Saute 3 to 5 minutes until the onions are tender.

Add bay leaf, sage and wine to the pan. Reduce wine by half, about 2 minutes. Add stock and pumpkin and stir to combine, stirring sauce until it bubbles gently. Return sausage to pan, reduce heat and stir in cream. Season the sauce with the cinnamon and nutmeg, then salt and pepper to taste. Simmer mixture 5 to 10 minutes to thicken sauce.

Return drained pasta to the pot you cooked it in. Remove the bay leaf from the sauce and pour the sausage pumpkin sauce over pasta. Combine sauce and pasta and toss over low heat for 1 minute. Garnish the pasta with lots of shaved cheese and fresh sage leaves.

We often make additional sauce, since we like creamy, saucy dishes. It's also nice to have extra.

"We're lucky enough to have Marlo,
but you can find a great local butcher
and start your own flavor tradition."

Recipe Notes

Recipe Notes

Pies, Desserts & Sweet-Natured Folk

Pie Potluck

Mary Beams is our accomplished pie baker and head pastry chef at The Pie Place Café. She comes from a family where pies are an art form, so it seemed only natural to ask her to talk about her pie-baking origins. Here's what Mary writes:

Pie-making as a creative art has been in my family for a few generations. My dad's grandfather owned a restaurant in a small town in Indiana; he sent his 15-year-old daughter off in a horse and buggy to the big city every Saturday to sell butter, eggs and the jams she made. She was instructed to eat the best dessert she could find, and to replicate it at home.

All week the sign in their window read: "Newest Dessert from Fort Wayne!" Most often those desserts were some form of pie.

My grandma's pies were legendary. She took pride in having the most sought-after pies at the church bake sales.

Dad liked to boast that he taught Mom how to bake pies – in a roundabout way. "I complained until she got them right." Mom's pies were another legend, and my brother and I were raised to believe that pie is the only dessert worth showing off, the only one worthy of a special occasion. On Mother's Day, my father and brother both celebrated their wives by baking pies from scratch. Fruit from the tree in my brother's backyard made juicy cherry pies; cherry was the men's favorite.

My parents belonged to a potluck group, begun during the Depression, which joined for dinner every month for more than 70 years. Mom and Dad met in that group. Of course, Mom brought pies when it was her turn for dessert. After many years, the potluckers primarily went to a restaurant for the meal, but dessert remained homemade, served at someone's home.

A year after Mom died, my Dad invited the potluck gang for dessert. He set the table with the best china and silver three days ahead of time. He made ice cream and baked cherry pie, getting up at 5 a.m. to make sure the pie came out all right and leaving enough time to do it over if it didn't suit his standards. On the dresser in the bedroom, he laid out Mom's favorite pieces of jewelry. After serving pie, ice cream and coffee, Dad invited the women to choose a piece of jewelry. They each came away with a necklace or bracelet that they remembered Mom wearing; each remarked about how close she felt that day and how proud Mom surely was of Dad and his great cherry pie. The party celebrated a new beginning, too. Asked about his future plans, Dad said, "Next week I have my cataract surgery, then I go to Florida to visit my brother. When I come back, I think I'll ask Alice for a date."

Alice had been his high school girlfriend; they did date for seven years until my dad passed away. Alice and Dad attended their 75th high school reunion together – both were still able to wear their letter sweaters.

Afterwards they went out for pie and coffee.

Pie Place Pie Dough

Since we were home pie bakers before we became professionals, we have experience with a variety of basic pie dough recipes. We inherited The Pie Place recipe, which seemed pretty well based on Crisco shortening's recipe, but was adapted for larger production. Over the years we've tweaked the recipe to get the best performance from our restaurant pies. Our café recipe would be of little use to the home pie baker because you have much more freedom to experiment. The following is an easy home recipe.

Assuming you may be new to pies, with the anxiety most first-time pie bakers hold, let me assure you that pie dough is easy and delicious, and it's enjoyable to practice refining dough to your own tastes.

Pie dough consists of flour, shortening, salt and water. It's true that certain conditions make the most tender and flaky crusts, but there is a lot of leeway within those conditions. Chilled shortening, cold water, fluffy flour all contribute to the basic chemistry of coating pellets of shortening with flour, binding them together with a little bit of moisture, rolling the dough flat and even, and counting on the baking to turn the moisture into steam. The flattened pellets, separated by the steam, create flakes of toasty, golden crust.

Though that is the chemistry of pie dough, and interesting to know, release yourself to the artistry of pie baking and allow the experience to be a joyful one. You'll do fine.

Makes 1 double-crust, 9-inch pie

Amount — Ingredients

1 cup	shortening, 1 stick butter plus 1/2 cup vegetable shortening makes the best combination. Slightly chilled can help in working the crust.
2 cups	flour
1 teaspoon	salt
1/3 cup	water

For double-crust pies

     Half-and-half, sugar and nutmeg, for brushing and sprinkling

Instructions

Cut the butter into small cubes; whisk the flour and salt together. Add the butter and shortening with a quick, light touch with a pinching motion, using your fingers, until the flour and shortening combine to form pea-size chunks. Add the water, holding back a little, and gently gather the flour mixture around the water until it holds together. Adjust in small increments with flour or more water as you go because the climate and temperature will affect how it all behaves. You want it to get just past crumbly for the best flavor. The more you handle the dough, the more it will be very solid and not flaky and tender.

When it is the right consistency, divide into two balls, one slightly larger than the other, if you are making one double-crust pie.

Hand form the dough balls into disks about 2 inches thick. Any cracks on the edges will cause irregular shapes when you roll out dough, so make sure the edges of the disk are smooth. Wrap the dough disks in plastic wrap and refrigerate it for at least 1 hour. The dough needs to rest to organize itself into your tasty crust, and needs to be chilled when you roll it.

Mary Beams, our pie maker extraordinaire. (photo by Claralyn Howard)

Have a pie pan ready. The best pans are glass or ceramic. If you are using a disposable tin, lightly grease it. Take out the largest disk, leaving the other in the refrigerator. Lightly flour your smooth counter surface and your rolling pin, and begin with even strokes to roll the dough. Use one hand as a pivot and the other to swing the pin in an arc. As the disk flattens, turn it frequently so it doesn't stick to the counter. If you roll in only one direction you will get a rectangle; by turning the dough often you will get a circle. As the dough enlarges, keep the end of the pin inside the edge of the dough to avoid making the outside crust edge too thin.

Center the rolled pie dough on the pie plate. Cut off the outer edge of

the dough to about 1 inch overhang, then roll the overhang under so it sits on top of the pie plate edge. If you are making a single-crust pie, you will crimp this by pressing a fork in a pattern around the edge or by pinching around the edge, keeping the crust edge an even thickness.

Preheat oven to 400° F.

To fully bake this single crust, prick the bottom and the sides a bit with a fork to let steam escape. Line the crust with parchment paper weighted with uncooked beans or rice or simply put another empty pie tin (disposable aluminum) atop this crust. Bake in the 400° oven for 15 minutes. Remove the weights, turn the pie crust around and bake for another 10 to 20 minutes, depending on how evenly your oven bakes, and how golden brown you want the crust. It should be golden enough for it to taste toasty, be crispy, flaky and tender. At The Pie Place Café, we put a pie tin on top, weighted with a small beach stone from the beach across the street – one of the many wonderful things about living on the North Shore. As a rule, we don't have a problem with it sticking.

Work the scraps back into the next disk or use the scraps to make "pie cookies" by sprinkling them with cinnamon sugar and baking them for about 15 minutes.

To make a double crust pie, arrange the bottom crust in the pie pan with a 1-inch crust overhang. Fill with the pie mixture and roll the second disk as you did the first. Make sure it's not too thick; 1/8 inch should be fine. Place it centered over the top of the pie and cut off any excess dough, leaving a 1-inch edge to match the bottom crust. Roll both crusts under along the pan edge and crimp. Brush the top with half-and-half, sprinkle with sugar and nutmeg to taste. Then cut small slits or a fancy pattern in the top of the crust to vent the steam.

Bake the pie according to its recipe directions.

The Pie Lady

In a life mechanized to a frantic crescendo, handmade things, wrought of the heart, transport us to a less complicated time when friends might sit around a kitchen table over a cup of coffee and a laugh. In those "olden days," as my grandma used to say before beginning any story about her girlhood, women baked crusty loaves of bread and flaky pies filled with wild berries. Life was hard then, but what mattered most to Grandma's family was the sharing of hearth, home-cooked food and friendship.

Tucked by the shore in the village of Grand Marais is a place where these simple pleasures still exist. Bread is baked in a brick oven, wooden boats are made in the way of early fishermen and knives, warm *nålbinding* mittens and birch baskets are crafted by hand.

Harley has a fine eye for carving . . . and for pie. (photo by Jeremy Chase)

North House Folk School is a treasure for us here. We've taken classes there, learned crafts nearly forgotten and met creative artisans eager to pass on their skills.

One can always tell when a North House carving instructor has dined at The Pie Place by the wood chips, scattered like new fallen snow, beneath the table.

One such carver, an expert in Scandinavian flat-plane carving, was doing a weeklong class when he began dropping into The Pie Place.

Day after day, Harley Refsal came to the restaurant, extolling the homemade soup and pie. Each day after his midday repast, he would ask to see a whole pie in all its flaky splendor. He'd study it intently, taking in its every nuance.

After days of chipping, carving, eating and painting, Harley unveiled "The Pie Lady," a small, handcarved wooden figure. Her chiseled features smiled, her countenance merry above the pie she held in her hands. I don't know about anyone else, but I could smell her fresh-baked offering – and I think Harley could, too.

Oh, and by the way, I believe The Pie Lady seems to have a vague resemblance to me.

Cherry Peach Pie

Harley loves pie so much that we're giving you two pie recipes with one story.

For this one, sweet juicy peaches lend themselves perfectly to lots of different fruit combinations. Don't be afraid to experiment. Some of our favorite pies started that way, and we're sure that yours will, too.

Serves 6

Amount — Ingredients

Amount	Ingredients
1 recipe (pg. 129)	double crust
3 cups	peaches, peeled, sliced
2 cups	sour cherries, pitted
1/2 teaspoon	almond extract
3 Tablespoons	cornstarch
1/2 cup	light brown sugar
1/2 cup	granulated sugar
Dash	salt
3 Tablespoons	butter, sliced in 8 pats
2 Tablespoons	half-and-half
	sugar, to sprinkle

Instructions

Preheat oven to 375° F.

Roll out dough into an 11-inch round on a lightly floured surface, using a floured rolling pin, and line a 9-inch pie pan with bottom crust.

In a large bowl, combine fruit, cornstarch, salt, almond extract and sugar. Place in the unbaked 9-inch pie shell. Dot with butter that's been cut into small pieces and cover with the top crust. Crimp and brush the top crust with half-and-half. Sprinkle with sugar to taste. Cut vents into the crust to vent steam. Place pie pan on a baking sheet.

Bake about 1 hour and 15 minutes, rotating halfway through to bake evenly. Pie is done when crust is golden and juices are thick and bubbly.

Plums, nectarines and apricots also work well in this recipe. If you want to experiment, or if you don't have peaches, fruits with pits go together well. Before baking, you can cut the crust into strips like those shown with "The Pie Lady" in this photo by Jeremy Chase for a fancy look.

Blackberry Peach Pie

Using peaches once again, this pie pairs them with blackberries for a summer-breeze refreshing combination. It's a double-crust pie, but here we added a whimsical North Woods touch by using a cookie cutter to place a dough bear on top.

Serves 6

Amount   Ingredients

1 recipe (pg. 129)   double crust (or with a bear flair)

Amount	Ingredients
5 cups	peaches, sliced
1 cup	blackberries
1-1/4 cup	sugar, plus some for sprinkling
3 Tablespoons	cornstarch
2 Tablespoons	butter
	half-and-half, for brushing
	nutmeg, for sprinkling

Instructions

Preheat oven to 375° F.

Place peaches and blackberries in an unbaked, un-crimped shell. Mix the sugar and cornstarch thoroughly. Sprinkle sugar and cornstarch mixture over the fruit. Dot with 2 tablespoons butter.

Roll out the top crust and place on the pie, tucking edges under and crimping the edges to seal. Brush with half-and-half, sprinkle with nutmeg. Cut out a bear shape from scraps of dough rolled very thin. Dip this in half-and-half and place in center of top crust. Sprinkle the whole top with sugar. Cut vents in top to let out steam.

Place on a baking sheet in the center of a preheated oven for about 1 hour, or until the juices are thick and bubbly, and the crust is golden brown. Each oven bakes differently; check the pie about halfway through, turn it around to compensate for any hot spots in your oven; after about one hour, check it frequently, 10-minute or so intervals, to make sure it doesn't burn.

"Each day after his midday repast,
he would ask to see a whole pie
in all its flaky splendor."

A Wee Word from Maggie

Whenever Maggie Gibbs arrives, I love thinking about how she has been coming here since before she was even born.

Maggie's mom and dad, Megan and Jeff Gibbs, and her grandparents, David and Linda Hoffman, have been eating at The Pie Place for years.

We've gotten to watch as wee Maggie grows up and now see her younger brother, D.J., too. Children remain our important guests at the restaurant. We've been privileged to see many grow into amazing adults and also get to watch as young parents, like Megan and Jeff, experience the joys of this sacred task of raising the next generation.

One of my favorite photos shows Maggie and her dad waiting to order a meal. Looking at it, I've imagined what baby Maggie might say about her visits here. It would go something like this:

"My name is Maggie. I like it when Kathy carries me around the restaurant, so I can check out what other people are eating. Can't wait until I can eat Big People food.

"One year my mommy and daddy had Valentine's Day at The Pie Place. It was a special dinner with flowers and candles and all that really neat stuff.

"They had the 'Lady and the Tramp' spaghetti dinner. Have you ever seen that movie Mr. Disney did about the two doggies that fell in love? They ate spaghetti and meatballs at an Italian restaurant and kissed in the middle. How romantic!

"Grandpa loves the cherry praline pie and the homemade bread. He takes a loaf home every time. My grandma raves about the salads, and my dad really goes for the maple pecan pie. I think that the future looks pretty good for me when I'm ready for my first meal here.

"Yes, someday soon I'll be sitting on a chair right next to Dad, reading the menu and ordering dinner all by myself. I can't wait!"

And we're so glad that we'll continue to be part of Maggie's growing up.

Maggie eating Big People food and earlier with Dad at the original Pie Place. (photos by Megan Gibbs)

Cherry Praline Pie

Maggie's grandpa loves our cherry praline pie and because Maggie loves him so very much, she and I decided it would be a great recipe for her story. This pie is a perfect way to say "I love you" on Valentine's Day or any day of the year.

Serves 6

Amount / Ingredients

1 recipe (pg. 129)   single crust

Praline Mix

1- 1/4 cups	all-purpose flour
1/2 cup	light brown sugar
3/4 cup	pecans, toasted and chopped
2 pinches	salt (about 1/4 teaspoon)
1 teaspoon	vanilla
2 Tablespoons	butter, melted

Maggie's little brother, D.J., getting acquainted with Kathy, (photo by Megan Gibbs).

Filling

1 can	cherry pie filling
1 cup	fresh or frozen sour cherries
1 teaspoon	almond extract

Instructions

Preheat oven to 375° F.

Melt butter on stove or in microwave. Blend in bowl with other praline mix ingredients.

Roll out dough into an 11-inch round on a lightly floured surface, using a floured rolling pin, and line a 9-inch pie pan with bottom crust. Sprinkle a thin layer – about 1/3 – of the praline mix on the bottom of an unbaked crimped pie shell.

Mix the cherries, cherry pie filling and almond extract together and then spoon into the shell on top of the layer of praline mix. Place the remaining praline mix on top of the filling, covering all the fruit out to the edges of the shell.

Bake in a 375° oven for 1 hour, until the top and crust are golden brown and the filling is bubbly.

Inspired by Maggie, we suggest that you serve this after a "Lady and the Tramp" spaghetti dinner, which can be an easy opening of jarred sauce (we like Newman's Marinara – sweet and garlicky), mixed with meatballs (frozen, from the butcher or homemade) and pasta. Kids can help make the meal. Light a few candles on the table, eat the spaghetti and pie and then pop "Lady and the Tramp" into the DVD player. It will be an enchanted evening.

A Pie Without Cheese ...

Every Sunday, my grandma would invite us over for dinner. Actually, she didn't need to invite us; we just all arrived, as she knew we would.

Grandma would put a creamy crocheted cloth on her massive oak table and set it with pale willowy green bone china from Germany. At each place setting was a tiny glass salt dip – the height of elegance in my 6-year-old eyes. I looked forward to our Sunday dinners.

Grandma's table was laden with crystal relish plates, a china tureen filled with rich, savory chicken and dumplings and flaky apple pie.

Walter, apple pie and a slice of cheese in our original Pie Place location. (photo by Jeremy Chase)

Being of Irish descent, we always had a strong pot of black tea.

When she brought the warm wedges of baked apple pie to the table, a few slices of sharp cheddar cheese always arrived as pie companions.

Such memories of good home-cooked food and the gathering of family and friends inspire us at The Pie Place. It's what we try to re-create in a restaurant setting.

Walter McCarthy, a mischievous soul, frequents the restaurant to satisfy his penchant for pie. His slice of pie, usually apple, must be accompanied by two ample slices of sharp cheddar cheese.

"A pie without cheese," quotes Walter, "is like a hug without a squeeze."

A few things are hallowed, never to be changed. For many folks like Walter and me, apple pie and cheese is one of them.

"A pie without cheese,
is like a hug without a squeeze."

Classic Apple Pie

Think of autumn – shorter, cooler days made for sweaters, forests ablaze with color, and crisp red apples clinging to branches laden and bending toward the ground. Eager to harvest the apples, we must wait until that first frost. Fall is a perfect time for the pleasures of apple butter on toast, warm and spicy applesauce and, of course, classic apple pie with, for those like Walter, a slice of cheese.

Serves 6

Amount   Ingredients

1 recipe (pg. 129)	double crust
7 cups	firm, tart apples, peeled, cored and sliced. We like Jonathans.
1 cup	sugar
2 Tablespoons	cornstarch
1/2 teaspoon	cinnamon
Dash & sprinkle	nutmeg
2 Tablespoons	butter
2 Tablespoons	half-and-half
	sugar, for sprinkling

Instructions

Preheat over to 375° F.

Roll out dough into an 11-inch round on a lightly floured surface, using a floured rolling pin, and line a 9-inch pie pan with bottom crust.

In a large bowl, mix the sugar, cornstarch, cinnamon, nutmeg and apples. Place in the unbaked pie shell. Dot with butter, cut into small pieces, and cover with the top crust. Crimp and brush the top lightly with half-and-half. Sprinkle with sugar and nutmeg to taste. Cut slits into the crust to vent steam. Place pie pan on a baking sheet.

Bake in the center of a 375° oven for 30 minutes. Turn the pie 180 degrees and bake until the crust is golden brown, juices are thick and bubbly, and the apples are soft when pierced with a paring knife. This could take anywhere from 20 to 40 more minutes, depending on your oven, how deep the pan is and how large the chunks of fruit are.

OUR MOCHA MOOSE

The restaurant's dining room is charged with anticipation. People arrive bearing all manner of things ... a guitar, a Bible, moose antlers, poetry books, papers covered with the innermost expressions of the heart.

In the dimly lit space, candles paint a creative ambience. A pastel drawing of a majestic moose standing in the forest hangs on the wall, artistic mascot of the evening.

We are hosting our annual "Mocha Moose Café."

It began in 1994 for just our family. The idea of a poetry performance night grew from our love of any excuse to celebrate each other and our artistic endeavors. We would gather, set the right mood for creativity and serve up coffee and dessert. Together this way, we spent cozy evenings writing and discussing life experiences. It was an opportunity to express our thoughts and feelings and to deepen and enrich our relationship as a family.

Our small community also has its annual Moose Madness festival honoring the majestic moose. So one year, we decided to open the doors to our "Mocha Moose Café" night. It was an instant success.

Those who join us can read a poem (or several if the muse is strong) and receive a slice of Mocha Moose Pie as reward. Often someone will select a poem from Walt Whitman, Robert Frost, Garrison Keillor's *Good Poems* or a favorite childhood poetry book. The resulting laughter, occasional tears and general camaraderie links

Mary Beams' blue moose is our Mocha Moose Café mascot.

us from year to year. One never knows who will come and what they will bring to the evening. And we're all on a first-name basis because sometimes we don't know last names.

Once a newlywed couple came to Mocha Moose – she a teacher and he recently back from Bosnia. She shared poems and pictures from her kindergarten class. We each took one and read it aloud, enjoying the innocent wisdom. He read poems about war, about experiencing the inconceivable. It was his plea to try another way and the reading brought him, I think, release and healing.

Another guest asked for a Bible and read I Corinthians 13: "And now these three remain: faith, hope and love. But the greatest of these is love." His voice, deep and rich as molasses, rang out like cymbals and the trueness of the words stirred our hearts.

Two hiking companions, who had spent the day walking in the woods and writing poems to bring to Mocha Moose, also brought in a shed moose antler they'd found. He surprised her that night with a poem that expressed his deep love.

One extremely shy fellow who had come to the gathering the year before got up to speak. "Last year I felt too afraid," he said, "but I've written a song, so I'll play it for you now." He then proceeded to play his guitar and sing an awesome song that he'd written. For shyness overcome and his courageous creativity, he earned his Mocha Moose Pie.

Young and old alike read poems. Lorenzo, Vaughn and their children love the written word. Their 9-year-old daughter read the first few lines of a poem about the loss of a beloved puppy, only to break out in tears in her mother's arms, so tender were those feelings.

Poetry links us to kindred spirits. Poetry strengthens and cleanses us.

Anna, sweet and articulate but profoundly shy, stood up before us with paper shaking from her fears. Then she proceeded to take us on a delightful journey of words, reciting the poems she had written while sitting on a rock beside Lake Superior. When she finished, the room erupted in a standing ovation. Away at college now, she will sit among us in spirit every year.

Kathy and Dennis always make us laugh with impish poems about "moose hunting" excursions to spot ungainly ungulates along the back roads of the Gunflint Trail.

Bob and Maureen, Pie Place regulars, bring their children and grandchildren. Their poems are from places we've never traveled. One year their grandson did a rap of things important to him – a musical road less traveled by our audience.

Our friend Buddy summed up the evening the best when he took a turn. He sat in a chair, nervously preparing to recite the lyrics to John Lennon's "Imagine." As he gazed out over the sea of faces before him, he took us all in, one by one, and then said with simple sincerity, "Isn't this beautiful?"

Mocha Moose Pie

Who doesn't like chocolate? One thing our family likes better than chocolate is the marriage of Katherine's homemade coffee ice cream and chocolate and voilà, a Mocha Moose Pie. This pie gets top honors every year at our Mocha Moose Café event. If you can't come to our annual poetry reading, we recommend you prepare this pie at home, gather a few friends (about seven to eat the whole pie with you), write and read some poems, and host your own Mocha Moose Café.

Serves 8

Amount · Ingredients

Amount	Ingredients
1	chocolate-cookie crumb crust, 9-inch, store-bought or see recipe pg. 151
1-2/3 cups	coffee ice cream, softened
1-2/3 cups	chocolate ice cream, softened
2 Tablespoons	Kahlua, optional
3/4 cup	toasted almonds, chopped, divided 1/2 cup for recipe, 1/4 cup for garnish
1/2 to 1 cup	hot fudge topping
2 cups	heavy cream, whipped

Instructions

Spread the coffee ice cream on the chocolate cookie crust. Freeze solid. Then spread a layer of chocolate ice cream, mixed with 2 tablespoons of Kahlua and 1/2 cup toasted chopped almonds, on top of the coffee ice cream layer. Freeze solid again.

To serve, soften slightly before cutting. Serve each piece drizzled with hot fudge and topped with whipped cream sprinkled with chopped toasted almonds.

THE ZANY FAMILY

Stephen, Patti, Suzannah, Jennifer and Hoss take a modern sleigh ride; Suzannah models her graduation garb with sister Jennifer. (photos from the Zany family collection)

Some of our favorite guests are a little zany.

Stephen and Patti Olsen and their daughters, Suzannah and Jennifer, playfully call themselves "the Zany Family." From our first encounter, they've enfolded us in a feeling that "we are so glad we found each other again."

Though they live in Minneapolis, it's common for them to drive all 265 miles to The Pie Place for lunch, visit for an hour or so, and then return home.

Their surprise appearances are like a homecoming. We hug, laugh even more and share what books we've been reading.

In the midst of it all, they "ooh and aah" over their food, relishing every morsel.

Daughter Suzannah adores our krab cakes, which is why Patti called for a "to go" order for Suzannah's high school graduation party. The family drove up to get them, had lunch and began the five-hour drive back home.

Suzannah does not live by krab cakes alone, of course. She, like her whole Zany Family, also loves pie. Whether they take home a whole pie, slices or some of each, they have their family favorites. Suzannah's is Cinnamon Peach Pie.

Soon after their last Pie Place pilgrimage, we received a DVD in the mail that was prepared by Patti. On it, she had captured one of their family visits to the North Shore, some time they spent at The Pie Place and her daughter Jennifer's wedding.

Stephen & Patti on the Grand Marais Harbor; Suzannah and Jennifer hanging out together; Suzannah savoring a meal as only she does; Suzannah & Hoss kayaking in the harbor.

Along with the DVD in the package, we found this note:
"We miss you Pie Place Family; just thought you'd like to have this."
We watched the video together that night after the restaurant closed.
We laughed, we cried (OK, I was the one who cried) and again felt connected to this family who has become part of our family.
If that's a little zany, then so be it.

"We miss you Pie Place Family; just thought you'd like to have this."

Cinnamon Peach Pie

When the fruits are in season, nothing beats a warm peachy pie. This unusual twist brings cinnamon for an unexpected flavor and a streusel topping that's sure to tickle the palate. As Suzannah says, "YUM!"

Serves 6

Amount   Ingredients

1 recipe (pg. 129)   single crust

Streusel topping

1-1/2 cups	all-purpose flour
1/2 cup	brown sugar
Pinch	salt
6 Tablespoons	melted butter

Filling

1-1/4 cups	sugar
3 Tablespoons	cornstarch
1/2 to 1 teaspoon	cinnamon, use to taste
6 cups	peaches, peeled and sliced, fresh or frozen
2 Tablespoons	butter

Instructions

For the streusel top: Toss the dry ingredients together, working out any brown sugar lumps. Pour the melted butter into the dry mix and toss together until mixture is crumbly.

Preheat oven to 375° F.

Roll out dough into an 11-inch round on a lightly floured surface, using a floured rolling pin, and line a 9-inch pie pan with bottom crust.

In a large bowl, mix the corn starch, cinnamon, sugar and peaches. Place in an unbaked pie shell. Dot fruit with butter cut into small pieces, then sprinkle the streusel evenly over the surface of the fruit filling. Crimp the edges decoratively. Place pie pan on a baking sheet.

Bake in center of 375° oven for 30 minutes; turn pie 180 degrees and bake until the crust is golden brown and the juices are thick and bubbly. This could take anywhere from 20 to 40 more minutes, depending on your oven.

"When the fruits are in season,
nothing beats a warm peachy pie."

THE MAN WHO PLANTS TREES

I and the tree are one.
Until the storms came
I thought my roots were shallow.
Now I know I can bend and not break.
– Doe Chase

Customer, waiter, planter of trees, friend …
this is the unfolding of Gavin in our life. We
came to know Gavin Stevens several years ago
upon his arrival in Grand Marais. He dined in
the restaurant with us from time to time, and his
devotion to eating pie quickly made him a regular.

One winter Gavin came to work with us as
a host/waiter/dishwasher/jack of all trades. He
did whatever we needed with a humble, willing
spirit. His humor and tales of travel entertained
us through the long, cold winter months. He
spoke of his visit to Rome and of spending
leisurely hours among the ruins of the ancient
Roman temples. He regaled us with tales of
eating Italian cuisine to his fill. Customers loved
Gavin as much as we did, and he fit perfectly
into the fabric of our life.

Gavin beside a painting of his passion. (photo by Jeremy Chase)

One night, as winter turned to spring, Gavin
asked if we'd like him to plant pine trees on our property. It was long our dream to have pine trees,
fruit trees and gardens of vegetables, herbs and flowers painting our landscape.

Trees, it turns out, are Gavin's passion. Like a modern-day Johnny Appleseed, he goes from place
to place planting and tending trees.

He worked diligently for two summers planting pines. We coaxed him into helping us plant
assorted fruit trees, maples and mountain ash, too.

Gavin possesses an intuitive nature, knowing when a certain tree isn't "happy" where it's been
planted. He heeds its wishes, moving it to a new location. More often than not, the little tree
responds with vigor and renewed growth.

In a world where trees are replaced with concrete and steel, where little thought is given to
destruction of habitat for our feathered and animal friends, it's heartening to know Gavin exists.

Our property is greener and more beautiful because of him. He's sensed where trees wanted to be
and created a new home for them and for us.

The trees will grow tall and strong, with boughs reaching to the sky. We may not be here to see
them in their splendor, but someone will.

Black Bottom Peanut Butter Mousse Pie

Our friend Gavin, a consummate chocolate lover, gives rave reviews to this combination of chocolate and peanut butter into one heavenly pie. Instead of the traditional graham-cracker crust, we have a twist – a crust made from crushed pretzels. It adds an interesting salty take on this sweet pie.

Serves 8

Amount   Ingredients

Pretzel Crust

Amount	Ingredients
2 cups	pretzel sticks, chopped or crushed fine, we like Rolled Gold Thin Sticks
3/4 cup	butter, melted
1/3 cup	light brown sugar, firmly packed

Filling

Amount	Ingredients
2 Tablespoons	sugar
1-1/3 cups	bittersweet or semisweet chocolate chips
2/3 cup	heavy cream (for chocolate layer)
1-3/4 cups	heavy cream, divided (for peanut butter layer)
2 Tablespoons	light corn syrup
2 teaspoons	vanilla extract, divided
1 cup	peanut butter chips
2 Tablespoons	creamy peanut butter (do not use old-fashioned, natural or freshly ground)

Instructions

Preheat oven to 350° F.

Make the crust: Reduce pretzels to fine crumbs in a food processor or crush in a plastic bag. Mix crumbs and sugar thoroughly, then add melted butter and mix until well blended. Put mix into a 9-inch pie pan and press firmly on the bottom and sides to make an even crust. Bake in a 350° oven for 10 to 12 minutes until crust is golden.

Combine chocolate chips, 2/3 cup heavy cream, corn syrup and 1 teaspoon vanilla in a microwave-safe bowl. Microwave on medium until chocolate softens (check often), about 3 minutes. Whisk until melted and smooth. Spread warm mixture over bottom of crust. Freeze 10 minutes.

Microwave peanut butter chips and 3/4 cup heavy cream in large microwave-safe bowl on medium heat at 15-second intervals just until chips soften, stirring often. Whisk in peanut butter and 1 teaspoon vanilla. Cool to barely lukewarm. Beat remaining 1 cup cream and 2 tablespoons sugar in medium bowl until very thick but not yet holding peaks; fold into peanut butter mixture in 3 additions. Spoon mousse over chocolate layer. Chill at least 1 hour and up to 1 day.

DICK AND JANE

"Run, Dick, run. See Jane run. Go, Spot, go." Bring back any childhood memories?

For many of us, Dick, Jane and Spot were as familiar as our childhood friends at school. We learned to read while envisioning these characters running across the pages of our reading book.

See ... Dick and Jane. (photo by Mary Beams)

For us at The Pie Place, Dick and Jane are still very real; they are among our favorite customers.

Friendly and full of life, it's like a walk through a spring forest when they arrive. They live confident that goodness endures in the world.

Dick and Jane Schirmacher also bring lively conversation and a joy for food. Their approach to food is much like their approach to life – eager, open and ready to try something new.

One summer evening, with the restaurant full and Jeremy and I hurrying to get food to the tables, Dick and Jane arrived. Bounding energetically through the front door and into the dining room, they exclaimed, "Do you remember who we are?"

Though I know their names as well as my own, in the harried pace of the moment, my mind went blank. Struggling to gain some composure, I blurted out, "Jack and Jill?"

Immediately my faux pas became clear to me. We looked at each other in startled surprise, and after a few brief beats, burst into gales of laughter.

From that day on, Dick and Jane became "aka Jack and Jill."

As you might have guessed, Dick and Jane love pie. True to their adventurous nature, they've tried nearly every pie on the menu, often eating several slices in one sitting. But don't let that fool you. They are fit and lean, eager to embark on their next hike up the hill and into the woods.

Oh, and they do have a dog that runs. His name is Spot.

Summer Fruit Pie

Eating pie all year around is, we think, "an essential need." But if you must choose one time of year to eat pie, pick the season when summer fruits are fresh, plump and plentiful. Dick and Jane gave this one a gold star (or an A+). It combines all our favorite berries and is sure to be a hit for that outdoor picnic or barbecue.

Serves 6

Amount   Ingredients

Amount	Ingredients
1 recipe (pg. 129)	double crust
2-1/2 cups	fresh peaches, peeled and cut into 1-inch slices
1-1/2 cups	tart cherries
1 cup	blueberries
1/2 cup	blackberries
1/2 cup	raspberries
3 Tablespoons	cornstarch
1-1/4 cups	sugar
2 Tablespoons	butter
2 Tablespoons	half-and-half
	sugar and nutmeg mixture

Instructions

Preheat oven to 375° F.

Roll out dough into an 11-inch round on a lightly floured surface, using a floured rolling pin and line a 9-inch pie pan with bottom crust.

In a large bowl, gently toss the fruits, cornstarch and sugar, then place in the unbaked pie shell. Dot with butter cut into small pieces and cover with the top crust. Crimp and brush the top lightly with half-and-half. Sprinkle with sugar and nutmeg to taste. Cut slits into the crust to vent steam. Place pie pan on a baking sheet.

Bake in the center of a preheated oven for 30 minutes. Turn pie 180 degrees and bake until the crust is golden brown and the juices are thick, and bubbly. This could take anywhere from 20 to 40 more minutes, depending on your oven, how deep the pan is, and how big the chunks of fruit are.

EAT PIE WITH ME

Grand Marais is a fine little town, brimming with people whose greatest joy is to do things to help others.

Our local library, the source of an amazing array of books, is staffed by such people. And we should know – as a family of readers, we count the library as one of the many blessings of living here.

Library staff member Elaine Erickson delights in locating obscure books not found on the shelves. If you want it, Elaine can and will find it – and with obvious joy as she sets about her search. When I don't have a book in mind, she'll direct me to new and thought-provoking volumes.

Elaine pauses by a painting of what she loves. Elaine also loves Grand Marais, where sailboats ply our summer waters. (Elaine by Mary Beams; sailboat by Jeremy Chase)

We've also come to know Elaine's penchant for pie, especially those that feature raspberries as a main ingredient. More than once, a slice of a signature raspberry pie or torte has appeared as if by magic on her desk at the library. It's just a little thank you for all she does for her bookie friends at The Pie Place.

One evening, while Elaine was having dinner at the restaurant, she revealed a personal tradition that surprised and delighted us.

She buys one of our whole pies, and then knocks on a friend's door and says, "Do you want to eat pie with me?"

Elaine became animated in the telling, and we got a new view of our library angel.

"I've created my own tradition," she explained. "I can share what I love and help someone else to have a brighter day."

Only once has someone declined her invitation, but, says Elaine, "Not to worry. I'll try again some other day."

Yes, Grand Marais is a great place to live.

Lemon Raspberry Pie

This is the perfect configuration of flavors – a chocolate crust swaddled with a light creamy lemon filling and garnished with fresh, plump raspberries. Cool and refreshing, this is a great summer dessert. For Elaine, this pie would be ripe for the sharing.

Serves 8

Amount   Ingredients

Chocolate-cookie Crumb Crust

2 cups	chocolate-cookie crumbs (wafers)
5 Tablespoons	butter, melted

Filling

1 package (8-ounce size)	cream cheese, softened
1 can (14 ounce size)	sweetened condensed milk
1/3 cup	fresh lemon juice (2 to 4 lemons, depending on size)
1 teaspoon	vanilla extract

Raspberries & Topping

1 pint	fresh raspberries, plus more for garnish (optional)
1 cup	heavy cream
2 Tablespoons	confectioner's sugar, sifted

Instructions

Make the crust: Crush crumbs in a plastic bag or pulse them in a food processor until very fine. In a medium-size bowl, mix the crumbs and melted butter thoroughly. Place mixture in a 9-inch pie pan and press crumbs firmly and evenly on the bottom and sides. Make certain the edge where the side meets the bottom is not too thick. For a softer crust, freeze at least an hour before filling. For a crispier crust, bake in a preheated 350° F oven for 8 minutes; cool completely before filling.

In a large bowl, beat the cream cheese and condensed milk together with an electric mixer on medium-high speed until smooth and fluffy, about 2 minutes. Add the lemon juice and continue to beat for 1 minute more. Blend in the vanilla. Pour the filling into the chilled pie shell and smooth the top with the back of a spoon. Cover with loosely tented aluminum foil and refrigerate for at least 2 hours, preferably longer (up to overnight).

Shortly before serving, scatter the raspberries evenly over the pie. Using a chilled medium-sized bowl and chilled beaters, beat the cream and confectioner's sugar until it holds soft peaks. Slice and serve, with a dollop of freshly whipped cream, garnishing with additional raspberries.

BEARS AND BEES

The Pie Place family has a dream of gardens full of fresh herbs, vegetables and edible flowers, of fruit trees from which we put up preserves, of brown farm-fresh eggs laid by contented chickens and ducks and of sweet golden honey produced by hives of industrious and pollinating honeybees.

We're taking steps into fulfilling our vision. We compost the vegetable scraps from the restaurant, creating rich, black dirt for our raised beds and soon-to-be-thriving vegetable gardens.

We've also become a family of avid beekeepers, parents as it were, for two hives of bees, who give their tiny but powerful all to produce the most glorious honey.

I began beekeeping 10 years ago, after reading *The Secret Life of Bees*, which awakened a dormant passion. As is always the case – when the student is ready, the teacher appears.

I called Gene Lehrke, a beekeeper of some 40 years. We began a conversation about bees and life in equal measure … a conversation that continues today.

A virtual bee encyclopedia, my mentor has become a friend born of sharing the trials, tribulations and unending joys of beekeeping. As Gene aptly put it during my first beekeeping season, "You've experienced 10 years of beekeeping in your first year. It seemed as if everything that could go wrong, did. The better to learn from, my dear."

One myth is that bears love honey. Actually, they love the bee brood. The forming larvae provide a great source of protein for a bear, hungry after a long winter's nap. Given my challenging first year, it wasn't a surprise that on one

A buzz with a new hive. (photo by Mary Beams)

particularly cold and rainy spring day – well, guess who came to dinner. The bear killed many of the bees, including the queen.

Gene, ever the teacher, helped me to understand what happens in a hive during times of mishaps and production. He prepared me for the fact that these bees, unable to keep warm enough with so few in the hive, would not survive the long, hard winter. It was a difficult lesson to accept.

Still, I was not deterred. I eagerly awaited our second bee season, receiving a portion of one of Gene's hives, enough to begin again. That year's honey harvest was just shy of 10 gallons. I thrilled to see the golden liquid spinning from the waxen combs. Gene was by my side, as always, helping to extract honey from the frames. Both of our faces were covered with honey and smiles.

Now we have enough honey to sell, a dream come true for one who has watched these tiny creatures work so diligently to give us this gift so perfect and pure.

The bees brought one more gift: a friend who taught me to see the world through wiser eyes and who gave me a glimpse into the secret life of bees.

Honey Pie

This pie would make bears, bees and my beekeeper friend Gene happy. Mary created this Honey Pie in honor of our hard working "little girls."

Serves 6 to 8

Amount   Ingredients

1 recipe (pg. 129)   single crust

2	eggs, beaten
2 cups	half-and-half
1/4 cup	honey
2/3 cup	sugar
3-1/2 Tablespoons	cornstarch
1 teaspoon	vanilla
2 Tablespoons	butter
1/4 teaspoon	salt

Instructions

Preheat oven to 375° F.

Roll out dough into an 11-inch round on a lightly floured surface, using a floured rolling pin and line a 9-inch pie pan with crust.

Trim excess dough and crimp edges decoratively. Cover the unbaked dough in the pan with parchment paper, making sure to include the sides of the crust as well. Weight the paper with beans or rice. Bake for 15 minutes. Take the partially baked crust from the oven, remove the weights and paper. Place the crust back into the oven and bake an additional 10 to 15 minutes, until golden brown. If the crust begins to puff up or a bubble forms, prick it with a fork and gently press flat. Remove from the oven and let cool.

Heat half-and-half to just under scalding. Remove from heat. Temper the beaten eggs by mixing them with 1/2 cup of the hot half-and-half, then pour mixture back into remaining half-and-half. Add honey.

In a medium saucepan, thoroughly mix liquid and sugar, cornstarch and salt (if butter is not salted, you might use more salt to taste). Cook over medium-high heat until it bubbles, stirring constantly. Cook another minute or so; the mixture will change from chalky to a bit of a sheen.

Remove from heat. Stir in butter and vanilla. Pour into baked and cooled crust. Lay plastic wrap directly onto full surface of the cream in order to avoid forming a skin. Chill at least 2 hours, until the filling is set. One serving suggestion is to top with whipped cream and a sprinkle of nutmeg or cinnamon.

THELMA AND LOU

The movie – and action – all begins with a waitress sweeping through the diner, a coffee pot in each hand ... a waitress like no other. Then Louise, frazzled by life's stress and strain, takes a much-needed vacation. Inviting her trusted friend Thelma to go along, their lives are changed forever.

We all should have someone in our life who's got our backs, someone who stands beside us in less-than-noble pursuits and in times that help us grow into the people we wish to become.

On the front lines of the restaurant business, where the unexpected is a daily occurrence and keeping your cool can be difficult, stands Lou.

Cindy Trieschmann, dubbed "Lou" by all of us who love her, has stood in the gap as a trusted employee and friend for 12 years. She, like the rest of us in this restaurant family, has cooked food from scratch, made pies and homemade bread, served food, washed dishes, cleaned and everything else required to keep a thriving restaurant running smoothly and efficiently.

So many mornings, the restaurant full to overflowing, Josh would be hovering over a 100-degree griddle preparing hundreds of eggs. Beside him would be Lou, plating eggs, toasting homemade bread, heating fruit compotes and filling containers with locally harvested maple syrup and homemade jam that she'd made.

Lou was there as we prepared and served our special Pie Place holiday dinners. I've lost count of the number of fresh turkeys we've stuffed, trussed and basted.

Catering was easier with Lou by my side – knowing she'd be there made an event for 200 "do-able" and less overwhelming.

Lou takes a break to sample what's on the menu. (photo by Mary Beams)

When we thought we couldn't muster the energy for another day, Lou would appear in the kitchen at 6 a.m. with a bag of "The World's Best Donuts," warm no less, from in town. After our first cup of coffee and a perfectly wonderful donut, we had the fortitude to go at it again.

Lou remembers those in our family who love dark chocolate, and those whose taste runs to milk chocolate –important knowledge when dispensing treats to keep the troops going.

She always remembers a birthday and always tucks a tin of my favorite beeswax and honey lip balm into my palm at the onset of another blustery winter. She's even helped me escort those tiny honey bees – they venture into the kitchen to see what's cookin' – back out the door and on their merry way.

On one rather hectic afternoon, we received a call from a new local establishment asking us to cater their grand opening. They wanted 40 pumpkin pies since it was a fall event.

"No problem," I said enthusiastically despite my weariness. "When is the opening?"

"Tomorrow."

I nearly fell on the floor. I turned and stared glassy-eyed at Lou, who was just walking out the door for the day. Then a look of sheer panic came on my face.

"We've just been asked to cater an event including 40 pumpkin pies for tomorrow. Would you be at all willing …"

Before I had even finished my desperate plea, Lou did an about-face and with a weary yet determined look said, "Would Thelma leave Louise?"

And there stood Lou, transformed into my Thelma and ready to back me up.

Speeding off in a green Ford Fairlane convertible did cross my mind, but instead we put the pedal to the metal in our kitchen.

"We just have to figure out what we're gonna do next," I said.

Lou stood beside me, shoulder to shoulder, as we cracked 120 eggs into bowls, combining them with enough pumpkin to start a pumpkin patch.

The next day, catering delivered and 40 pumpkin pies strewn with fluttering leaves fashioned of pie dough (we must have been insane), one eager guest exclaimed, "The Pie Place is amazing! How did you manage all this?"

All I need is Lou to be my Thelma.

"All I need is Lou to be my Thelma."

Pumpkin Praline Pie

We've been pumpkin pie purists, always loving that old-fashioned, spicy flavor and adhering to our pumpkin-pie roots inherited from grandmothers and mothers. But just imagine for a minute, if there was a layer of crunchy caramelized pecan nestled underneath all that pumpkin. This pie is worth breaking that tradition. No wonder whenever we make it, Lou gives us her mischievous grin. It's one of her favorites.

Serves 6

Amount   Ingredients

1 recipe (pg. 129)   single crust

Praline Mix

4 Tablespoons	butter
1/2 cup	pecan pieces, toasted
1/3 cup	brown sugar

Basic Pumpkin Pie Filling

3/4 cup	granulated sugar
1/2 teaspoon	salt
1 teaspoon	cinnamon
1/2 teaspoon	ground ginger
1/4 teaspoon	ground cloves
2	eggs
1 can (15-ounce size)	solid pack pumpkin (not the pie filling)
1 can (14-ounce size)	evaporated milk

Brown-sugar Whipped Cream

2 cups	heavy cream
1/4 cup	brown sugar
1 teaspoon	vanilla extract

Instructions

Preheat oven to 325° F.

Roll out dough into an 11-inch round on a lightly floured surface, using a floured rolling pin, and line a 9-inch pie pan with bottom crust. Crimp edges.

Make the praline: Toast the pecan pieces in a 325° oven for 6 to 8 minutes. In a small saucepan, cook the butter, toasted pecans and brown sugar until sugar is melted and mixture is blended. Cool slightly.

Make the filling: Mix the granulated sugar, salt and spices; add the eggs, pumpkin and evaporated milk.

Assemble the pie: Pour the cooked praline into the pie shell and spread it evenly to cover the bottom. Top with pumpkin mixture. Bake at 325° until the mixture jiggles only slightly, or until a toothpick inserted into the center comes out clean, about 50 minutes to one hour.

We suggest serving it with a dollop of brown-sugar whipped cream made from 2 cups heavy cream, 1/4 cup brown sugar, 1 teaspoon vanilla and beaten in a medium bowl until stiff peaks form.

CROSSING BORDERS

Moving northeast from Grand Marais, the rugged Lake Superior shoreline meanders gently to Grand Portage and beyond.

Once over the border, the majestic Canadian forest and Nor'wester Mountains surround you before you reach another blue expanse of the Great Lake near Thunder Bay. Upper Minnesota and Canada share in the grandeur of this majestic vista, and the border seems only an imagined barrier between us and our neighbors.

The Pie Place has many wonderful customers and friends from Canada.

Thunder Bay, a mere one-hour drive from the U.S. border, seems like a "stone's throw" away. It is common for Ontario folks to drive to Grand Marais for lunch and a day of browsing in the local shops.

Eric and Sue Imperius frequent The Pie Place, enjoying the drive along the shore and calling ahead to order fresh-baked scones to take home.

In true Canadian spirit, they are warm, friendly and giving people. They frequently bring us an incredible edible gift made in Canada. Called "Clodhoppers," it is a snack made of crunchy chocolate-covered graham-wafer clusters that we must hide from ourselves for fear of eating the whole bag in one sitting.

On September 11, 2001, when terrorists crashed planes into the twin towers of the World Trade Center in New York City, we and the rest of the nation watched in horror and disbelief at the explosions and ultimate collapse of the towers.

Eric and Sue drop in from Thunder Bay. (photo by Jeremy Chase)

Customers flocked to the restaurant that day, almost as if to seek solace and the comfort of familiar faces and food. Mostly we all listened and even in The Pie Place, food was almost an afterthought for those who came.

The following day again seemed surreal, as we moved through the day, serving our guests. That afternoon, while helping to prepare dinner, I looked up to see two people peering through the kitchen door. There stood Eric and Sue; they had come from Thunder Bay to let us know how sorry they were about what had happened and to ask what they could do.

In that moment, the grief and confusion of the last few days fell away, as the truth of common humanity and a good and loving world stood before me.

"What can you do?" I said, appreciating their trip across that border. "You've already done it!"

French Canadian Maple Syrup Pie

In honor of our Canadian neighbors, friends and frequent guests, we present this pie honoring the ambrosial sap that flows abundantly from maple trees in the surrounding forests and is used to produce sweet, amber syrup. We believe it's worth a border crossing for those like Eric and Sue, who have a bit of a sweet tooth.

Serves 6

Amount   Ingredients

1 recipe (pg. 129)   single crust

Pie Filling

Amount	Ingredient
1-1/2 cups	light brown sugar, packed
pinch	salt
3 large	eggs, at room temperature
2/3 cup	heavy cream
1/2 cup	pure maple syrup, preferably dark amber or grade B
1 teaspoon	vanilla extract
2 teaspoons	butter, unsalted, melted
	Serve with crème fraîche or unsweetened whipped cream

Instructions

Preheat oven to 350° F.

Roll out dough into an 11-inch round, on a lightly floured surface with a floured rolling pin, and fit into a 9-inch pie pan. Trim excess dough and crimp edges decoratively.

Whisk together brown sugar, salt and eggs until creamy. Add heavy cream, syrup, vanilla and butter, then whisk until smooth. Pour filling into unbaked pie shell.

Bake pie in lower third of oven until pastry is golden and filling is set, puffed and looks slightly dry, 50 to 60 minutes. (Filling can be slightly jiggly and will set further as it cools.) Cool on a rack to room temperature. Serve with unsweetened whipped cream.

For Allah

Summers are busy at The Pie Place, with Grand Marais and the Gunflint Trail being popular destinations for vacationing families who hope to escape the hectic pace of city life.

In communities who serve visitors, many establishments employ young people from other countries to assist during summer's influx of guests.

Grand Marais is no exception, and through the years The Pie Place has employed young people from Jamaica, Egypt, Peru, Romania, Macedonia, Russia, England, The Dominican Republic and Spain.

We enjoy these young, energetic and hard-working university students, learning about life in other countries, and we establish deep connections and friendships with them. They become an integral part of life at The Pie Place, assisting us to serve the summertime adventurers.

A group of students from Turkey made indelible marks on our lives.

Murat, a veterinary student, came to the United States to experience a different culture and expand his grasp of the English language. He soon won our hearts and those of our customers.

Kayhan, too, became a beloved member of The Pie Place Family, working with us in every imaginable capacity. Energetic and conscientious, his charm and loving spirit have enhanced our lives and those of our guests. Friendship knows no boundaries, and Turkey seems not so far when they are here. Kayhan's diligence, sweet and positive spirit and attention to detail made him an integral member of our team.

Hanging out together are The Pie Place crew of Jeremy, Kayhan, Seyfe and Ben. (photo by Nadya Shkurdyuk)

They were joined, too, by Esref and Yavuz, also hard and willing workers.

One day, after rolling silverware meticulously in cloth napkins for dinner, Murat began to vacuum the carpet and straighten chairs, putting all in beautiful order.

I thanked him, letting him know that his attention to detail was important and meant a lot to us. He looked at me, puzzled. "You are most welcome, but I do it for Allah!"

God is in the details, and those words are spoken the world over in many different ways.

Ramadan, called Ramazan in Turkey, is the 30-day Islamic holy month celebrated in all Muslim countries. It is a sacred and special time of fasting, prayer and celebration.

During the month of Ramazan, Istanbul's Blue Mosque is illuminated in lights with the message: Sefaat Yaresul Allah! ("Intercede for us, O prophet of God")

Murat and his friends were in Grand Marais during Ramazan. As with any significant holiday, holy day, it is difficult to be apart from family and those you love. Murat expressed sadness at not being able to celebrate Ramazan with his father, mother and family with whom he is very close.

He and his friends asked if they could have their special Ramazan dinner at The Pie Place. We decided to surprise them with a traditional Ramazan dinner.

Fasting is required from sunrise to sunset during Ramazan. The feasting begins with a ceremonial "breaking of the fast" called Iftar. It includes flat pita bread, soup, pickled olives, feta cheese and cups of strong black tea.

Imagine four young men who hadn't eaten since 4 o'clock that morning. Imagine our joy at presenting and theirs at receiving Iftar. They devoured their food with relish.

After dinner, during which a full loaf of bread was consumed, dessert was served. Baklava, a traditional pastry, is much loved by the Turkish people. Containing layer upon layer of phyllo dough, honey and walnuts, it is painstaking to make.

While shopping a few days before the celebration, Katherine found enough of this honey-drenched delicacy for all of our young friends. God is indeed great!

Esref brought traditional Turkish music, which is played during their holy days, and asked if it would be okay to play it.

We asked those dining in the restaurant if they would mind, explaining that Murat and his friends were celebrating Ramazan. Not only were our other guests excited to hear the music, each person approached Murat's table wishing 'Happy Ramazan' to each one.

At night's end, with smiles on their faces, and tears in their eyes, our newfound friends announced with great passion that this meal had truly been the highlight of their trip to America – one that they would remember fondly forever.

"We enjoy these young, energetic and hard-working university students."

Rice Pudding

Rice pudding seems to be popular worldwide. Sütlaç, the Turkish word for rice pudding, is much loved by our friends from Istanbul. They say that their grandmothers, mothers and aunts make it in large pots during Ramazan and for other holy days. We've started the same tradition by serving it every year at our Ramazan dinner, where we host all the Muslim students who come to Grand Marais to work. Thanks to gifts from friends, we have the luxury of sprinkling our sütlaç with Turkish cinnamon from the bazaars of Istanbul, but any cinnamon is a nice touch.

Serves 6

Amount — Ingredients

Amount	Ingredients
4 cups	whole milk
3/4 cup	sugar
1/2 cup	long-grain basmati rice
1-1/2 cups	water
4 Tablespoons	cornstarch
1	egg yolk

Instructions

In a big pot, add milk and sugar, stir and bring to boil, then reduce heat to low and simmer.

Wash and drain the rice and put it into a medium pot with the water. After bringing it to a boil, simmer until rice is very tender and water is absorbed. Add more water if necessary while cooking.

When rice is cooked, with a back of a wooden spoon, mash the rice until half of it is crushed. Add to a simmering milk-sugar mixture and stir.

In a small bowl, stir cornstarch and egg yolk with a little water until smooth. Pour in a thin stream into the milk and rice mixture, stirring constantly. Cook 2 to 3 minutes more until thickened.

Pour the rice into serving cups. Let it cool, and then chill in the refrigerator. Before serving, sprinkle with a little cinnamon.

Kayhan's fiancée, Deniz, joins the celebration by serving sütlaç and other Turkish delights at our Ramazan dinner prepared for our visiting friends from Turkey and other countries. (photo by Kathy Rice)

LOVE SONG

Here at The Pie Place, we have a great appetite for Valentine's Day and it's our tradition to prepare and serve an intimate, sumptuous dinner in celebration of love.

We say "I Love You" with the flowers, candles and homemade truffles that grace the tables, awaiting the arrival of our guests.

Though each year we try to create a wonderful, unique experience, one Valentine's Day stands out among the rest.

Our guests had arrived. Soft music mingled with the aroma of prime rib, and candlelight set faces aglow. A group of women, traveling back to Ontario from a singing competition in the Twin Cities, stopped at the restaurant for a late lunch.

Jeremy, who was waiting on their table, asked if they would sing for us. Soon strains of beautiful voices merging in harmonic splendor drifted into the kitchen, drawing us into the dining room. There, 12 women – the "Sounds of Superior" – were flowing from table to table.

Some couples were holding hands, while others sang along. Requests for favorite songs were sung with enthusiasm, and there was more than one misty eye in the place.

Love is conveyed in many ways – a knowing look between two people, a gentle touch, food prepared and shared, a kind, encouraging word … and sometimes, love songs sung to strangers who, as if by magic, become friends.

Decorations make these cookies go with any holiday. (photo by Jeremy Chase)

164

Traditional Sugar Cookies

Often baked for holidays, we humbly suggest whipping up a batch of sugar cookies for any time of year. Let the children of your family help to decorate with traditional confectioner's sugar icing, tinted in the hues of the season. That's baking memories for certain.

Makes 3 to 4 dozen

Amount — Ingredients

Amount	Ingredients
1 cup	butter, softened
1/2 cup	sugar
1	egg
2 teaspoons	vanilla extract
2-1/2 cups	sifted all-purpose flour
1/2 teaspoon	baking powder
1/8 teaspoon	salt

Frosting

1 Tablespoon	butter, softened
1-1/2 cups	confectioner's sugar
1/2 teaspoon	vanilla extract
	milk, adding to desired consistency, but you don't want your frosting too thick or too thin

Instructions

Preheat oven to 350° F.

To make the cookies, cream the butter and sugar together. Add the egg and vanilla and mix well. Sift together the dry ingredients and slowly add to the butter mixture. Combine until a dough is formed. If the dough is too wet, add up to an additional 1/2 cup of flour.

Put one quarter of the dough onto a floured surface. Sprinkle the top of the dough with flour. Using a rolling pin, roll out the dough until it is 1/8-inch thick. Cut out desired shapes with cookie cutters and place on an ungreased cookie sheet. Repeat until all the dough has been used.

Bake at 350° for 8 to 10 minutes or until lightly browned on the edges. Remove cookies. When they have cooled, you can frost them.

To prepare frosting, cream together the butter and confectioner's sugar. Add the vanilla and mix well. Pour in milk, 1 teaspoon at a time until you have a spreadable consistency. Frost the cooled cookies and decorate as desired. The frosting can be made several hours before the cookies are baked and should be kept in the refrigerator. Allow time for the frosting to soften for use.

BIRTHDAY PIE

From the horizon, you go beyond the edge of the world to the sky and beyond that to the unknown. I always imagine, in a certain surrealist way, that I am there. I like to imagine it is real.
– George Morrison, Turning the Feather Around

We first met Mike Morrison when we owned our art gallery and gift store, Northern Impulses. The gallery, housed in an historic log building with a massive stone fireplace, clung to the shore of Lake Superior.

Local folks came to look at art, buy a special gift, or talk … the way people in a small community love to do.

We were visited by young people who dropped in after school, elderly folks quenching the thirst for company that loneliness brings, and others simply drawn to beauty and things of the heart. We spent companionable moments reminiscing, speaking of dreams and expressing thoughts and stirrings of the heart.

Mike came into Northern Impulses while in town to get provisions for the week.

Quiet at first impression, he studied the subtle colors in a pastel hanging on the rough log wall. Then he turned to me with a knowing look in his eyes.

"Great framing job," he said.

The small beacon of the Grand Marais harbor lighthouse is a familiar landmark for local people. (photo by Nadya Shkurdyuk)

Mike went on to explain: "My brother George is an artist. I'm not very creative myself, but I make the frames for his paintings."

Making frames and skillfully presenting another's work is an art form, I assured him, adding that he should never underestimate his contribution.

His face lit up then, and we became friends from that moment on.

Mike dropped in frequently, and we discussed art and life in equal measure.

He also became a regular customer at The Pie Place, where we soon learned of his fondness for blueberry pie. He especially liked it when we could get wild blueberries. Tiny, sweet morsels, their hold on him was irresistible.

One day he appeared at the restaurant announcing that it was his birthday and that he was "spending a night in town to celebrate." He planned to stay at the East Bay Hotel and have his birthday dinner at The Pie Place.

Though weakened by a recent heart attack, Mike enjoyed his dinner, taking pleasure in every bite.

"The Witch Tree" by Mary Lear celebrates the Spirit Little Cedar, a 400-year-old neighbor along the Lake Superior shore that is sacred for the Ojibwe people.

He was eager for the final course, blueberry pie, but alas …

"I haven't eaten this much in ages," he admitted contentedly. "But I'm too full for dessert. I'll take my birthday pie with me for a little snack later."

I placed a slice of blueberry pie in a container with a blue birthday candle (I can't help myself) and a note: "Happy Birthday, Mike. We love you!"

I handed it to him and he opened the box to peer inside, a look of gustatory anticipation on his face. Spying the birthday candle, he looked at me, eyes moist. He took my hand in his, lifted it to his lips and, without reservation, kissed it tenderly.

"Happy birthday, Mike," I said, choking back tears myself. "Thank you for sharing your special day with us."

That was the last time we saw Mike. Though he'd invited us to his cabin in Grand Portage to see some of his brother's paintings, Mike passed away before we would get there.

He seemed ready for his passing into another world.

He was found lying on his bed, dressed in his best suit, a rosary clasped in his hands and cherished Anishinaabe artifacts placed around him. A serene look on his face, I think he had joined his brother George on the other side.

Who knows what beauty they are creating together there.

Pie Place Blueberry Pie

Of course Mike's birthday pie would be blueberry. He loved anything with blueberries and often recounted fond memories of blueberry picking in the woods surrounding Grand Portage with his brothers and sisters. Late summer and blueberry picking go hand in hand up in these parts, with many people never revealing their favorite berry-picking spots.

Serves 6

Amount   Ingredients

Amount	Ingredients
1 recipe (pg. 129)	double crust
1 cup	sugar
3 Tablespoons	cornstarch
1/8 teaspoon	almond extract
1 Tablespoon	lemon juice
4-1/2 cups	blueberries, fresh or frozen
2 Tablespoons	butter
2 Tablespoons	half-and-half
	sugar and nutmeg

Instructions

Preheat oven to 375° F.

Roll out dough into an 11-inch rounds on a lightly floured surface, using a floured rolling pin, and line a 9-inch pie pan with bottom crust.

In a large bowl, mix the sugar, cornstarch, almond extract, lemon juice and blueberries and place in the unbaked pie shell. Dot with butter, cut into small pieces, and cover with the top crust. Crimp and brush the top lightly with half-and-half. Sprinkle with sugar and nutmeg to taste. Cut slits into the crust to vent steam. Place pie pan on a baking sheet.

Bake in the center of a 375° oven for 30 minutes. Turn the pie 180 degrees and bake until the crust is golden brown, and the juices are thick, and bubbly. This could take anywhere from 20 to 40 minutes more, depending upon your oven.

"He especially liked it when we could get wild blueberries. Tiny, sweet morsels, their hold on him was irresistible."

Recipe Notes

Recipe Notes

LETTING GO, GOING ON

May you find us worthy to place among us those whom you would have us serve.
– Cheryl Polson

Letting go isn't always easy. Yet as a family, we've learned that releasing the old, no matter how safe and familiar it may seem, creates the pathway for a new and exciting life. James Taylor refers to it as a "daring daylight escape." Not easy, but necessary if one is to grow. In short, we decided to follow our dream of living in a beautiful and remote area, where we could make art and live a simpler life.

Our story started nearly 18 years ago when we pulled up roots, let go of the life we had all known and moved to Grand Marais from DeKalb, Illinois.

Our love of the North Woods and the inspiration it provides us as artists drew us to Grand Marais. As we settled into this little community nestled along the shore of Lake Superior, we began to feel that we had truly found home. We started an art gallery.

Not long after, fate cast a card we hadn't foreseen. The Pie Place became available. Eagerly, though tentatively, we rolled up our culinary sleeves and began to build the restaurant that our guests now love and to which they come home. As we embarked on our journey, food became another creative outlet for our family. The Pie Place became an extension of the "home" we had grown to love ... a way to share with those who came to dine at our restaurant, all that this area has to offer.

Many wonderful meals were planned, prepared, served and savored in our little restaurant on top of

We feel we have found a true home in Grand Marais. (photo by Nadya Shkurdyuk)

The original home of The Pie Place just on the edge of Grand Marais. (photo by Phil Westine)

the hill at the edge of Grand Marais. So many memories, etched in our hearts, remain as we read these stories from 17 years of serving those who have become friends, a true extension of our Pie Place family.

At times, we'd get discouraged. Bone tired and seemingly unable to go on, Cheryl would say, "Don't look at the building, look at what we are building." These words inspired us to carry on. But what was it we were building? Anyone can cook food, can't they?

Little by little, it became clear to us, and I hope to our guests, that we were serving more than food in that little white bungalow. They seemed to find sustenance of body and soul, and we saw the unfolding of a plan greater than any we'd imagined. I like to think that The Pie Place became a home away from home for our guests who traveled to the North Shore.

We've watched children grow from toddlers to teens. We've celebrated birthdays, anniversaries, retirements and holidays. We've mourned the passing of dear friends and loved ones. We've tried to be a place where people could say, "I need to talk," and would know that someone would take the time and the love to do just that.

All these were necessary ingredients in what we were building – a life well lived and a restaurant that served more than just food. Often it's only when you turn to look back that you realize the fullness of what the experience meant.

A little over a year ago, we were called once again to let go of a part of the life we've known. We moved our little restaurant on the hill to a new in-town location with a stunning view of the harbor and lighthouse – and room to feed even more people. We've left behind the old building, but who we are and what we believe in moved with us into The Pie Place Café.

Again, we rolled up our chef-ly sleeves, creating new recipes that merged with those tried and true flavors of our origins. Life is a work in progress, and the life of a restaurant isn't much different.

We've learned so many things over the last 17 years as a restaurant family. We've learned about commitment, service to others, hard work and striving for excellence. We learned about new beginnings. Most of all, we've learned about love. It is truly our essential ingredient.

ABOUT THE AUTHORS

This book has my name, Kathy Rice, on the cover, but truth be known there are multiple "authors" to this work. As with any small, family-owned restaurant, all of us have rolled up our culinary sleeves to do whatever was required to keep The Pie Place Café running smoothly. Rolling pie shells and making pies to baking bread to preparing the meals to picking and arranging flowers, cleaning, sweeping, mopping and, yes, doing dishes – we've all pitched in to help.

That is the case with pulling together this book and these recipes. We each bring our special gifts to The Pie Place Café and we are all "authors." Let me introduce you to the family:

I'll start with one who has left us but remains so vital to our daily work and lives. Cheryl Polson, with her gift of envisioning the ultimate experience, created a weekly changing menu. By bringing together a flavorful array of foods, she orchestrated memorable meals. Her evening repasts were a favorite among our guests: a meal with which they could linger, take in all the subtle flavors of each course and enjoy a few leisurely hours of food and conversation. Food was art for Cheryl, her way of expressing the passion she had for cooking, for people and an enchanted life.

The Pie Place family, from left: Josh, Kathy, Mary L., Clare, Mary B., Katherine, Ben, Jeremy. (photo by Nadya Shkurdyuk)

Mary Lear, a pastel artist, brings artistic sensibility to food. She and Cheryl would pore over cookbooks (of which we have many) and food magazines for ideas and inspiration. Mary is a chef in the restaurant, too, with a creative eye when it comes to planning menus, cooking and presenting food. She brings her interior design background to catering and special events. Her attention to detail and those special touches delight the senses.

Clare Shaw spends countless hours pulling recipes, typing, copying and putting together our menus. When a restaurant changes its menu every week, this is no small task. Her management skills contribute to the smooth functioning of The Pie Place Café, relative to advertising, human relations and systems organization.

Over the years, Josh Rice, Ben Zang and I have lent our culinary hands to preparing food. Cheryl once referred to Josh as an "ever-aspiring Renaissance man; he comes to everything he does from an artistic sensibility, whether lathing a beautifully turned wooden bowl or pan sautéing a duck breast that will be dressed in blackberry sauce." Ben has created meals with complex flavors and visual interest, pairing each with the perfect wine to enhance each dish. His signature salsa is a favorite among our guests who like a punch for their palate. I love dressings and sauces and seem to have an innate sense of how to combine fresh herbs, oils, vinegars, wine and stocks to create the perfect accompaniment to a dish. Cheryl used to say, "I want it to taste like this. I'll leave it up to you to create it." Doing just that was and is one of my culinary joys. Cooking for people I love is what I love best!

Mary Beams, filmmaker, painter and jewelry artist, and Katherine Goertz, an amazing fiber artist (weaver, quilter and knitter), bring their passion and visual refinement to the flaky, succulent pies, delicate, flavorful scones and crusty homemade bread. There is such artistry in baking, and they meld their artistic sensibility into that art. For Mary, pie is art and a family tradition. Katherine, enthralled with all things chocolate, has made English toffee and truffles to live for!

Jeremy Chase, energetic and full of enthusiasm for life, is a waiter extraordinaire. His quick wit and easy charm bring smiles and laughter to those who come to dine at The Pie Place Café. He enlivens conversation with our guests, seasoning their experience with thoughtful humor and much entertainment. As a musician, Jeremy has brought the gift of music to dinner parties and celebrations at the restaurant. As a photographer, he brings new vision, and his images are among those sprinkled with flavorful seasoning throughout this book.

I'm pleased to be able to introduce these members of my family and my "co-authors" for this work. I hope one day you'll be able to come in and meet us in person.

We'll wait for you by the Big Lake's shore.

"All of us have rolled up our culinary sleeves to do whatever was required."

INDEX
INGREDIENTS & RECIPES

PEOPLE, PLACES & THINGS

Section Opening Photos

Photographers

From Lake Superior Port Cities Inc.

Lake Superior Magazine
A bimonthly, regional publication covering the
shores along Michigan, Minnesota, Wisconsin
and Ontario

Lake Superior Travel Guide
An annually updated mile-by-mile guide

**Lake Superior, The Ultimate Guide to the
Region – Second Edition**
Softcover: ISBN 978-0-942235-97-5

Hugh E. Bishop:
The Night the Fitz Went Down
Softcover: ISBN 978-0-942235-37-1

**By Water and Rail: A History of
Lake County, Minnesota**
Hardcover: ISBN 978-0-942235-48-7
Softcover: ISBN 978-0-942235-42-5

Haunted Lake Superior
Softcover: ISBN 978-0-942235-55-5

Haunted Minnesota
Softcover: ISBN 978-0-942235-71-5

Beryl Singleton Bissell:
A View of the Lake
Softcover: ISBN 978-0-942235-74-6

Bonnie Dahl:
**Bonnie Dahl's Superior Way,
Fourth Edition**
Softcover: ISBN 978-0-942235-92-0

Joy Morgan Dey, Nikki Johnson:
Agate: What Good Is a Moose?
Hardcover: ISBN 978-0-942235-73-9

Daniel R. Fountain:
**Michigan Gold,
Mining in the Upper Peninsula**
Softcover: ISBN 978-0-942235-15-9

Chuck Frederick:
Spirit of the Lights
Softcover: ISBN 978-0-942235-11-1

Marvin G. Lamppa:
Minnesota's Iron Country
Softcover: ISBN 978-0-942235-56-2

Daniel Lenihan:
**Shipwrecks of
Isle Royale National Park**
Softcover: ISBN 978-0-942235-18-0

Betty Lessard:
Betty's Pies Favorite Recipes
Softcover: ISBN 978-0-942235-50-0

Mike Link & Kate Crowley:
**Going Full Circle:
A 1,555-mile Walk Around the
World's Largest Lake**
Softcover: ISBN 978-0-942235-23-4

James R. Marshall:
**Shipwrecks of Lake Superior,
Second Edition**
Softcover: ISBN 978-0-942235-67-8

**Lake Superior Journal:
Views from the Bridge**
Softcover: ISBN 978-0-942235-40-1

Kathy Rice:
**The Pie Place Cookbook:
Food & Stories Seasoned
by the North Shore**
Softcover: ISBN 978-1-938229-04-6

Howard Sivertson
**Driftwood:
Stories Picked Up Along the Shore**
Hardcover: ISBN 978-0-942235-91-3

**Schooners, Skiffs & Steamships:
Stories along Lake Superior's Water Trails**
Hardcover: ISBN 978-0-942235-51-7

Tales of the Old North Shore
Hardcover: ISBN 978-0-942235-29-6

The Illustrated Voyageur
Hardcover: ISBN 978-0-942235-43-2

**Once Upon an Isle:
The Story of Fishing Families
on Isle Royale**
Hardcover: ISBN 978-0-962436-93-2

Frederick Stonehouse:
**Wreck Ashore: United States
Life-Saving Service,
Legendary Heroes of the
Great Lakes**
Softcover: ISBN 978-0-942235-58-6

Shipwreck of the Mesquite
Softcover: ISBN 978-0-942235-10-4

Haunted Lakes (the original)
Softcover: ISBN 978-0-942235-30-2

Haunted Lakes II
Softcover: ISBN 978-0-942235-39-5

Haunted Lake Michigan
Softcover: ISBN 978-0-942235-72-2

Haunted Lake Huron
Softcover: ISBN 978-0-942235-79-1

Julius F. Wolff Jr.:
**Julius F. Wolff Jr.'s
Lake Superior Shipwrecks**
Hardcover: ISBN 978-0-942235-02-9
Softcover: ISBN 978-0-942235-01-2

www.LakeSuperior.com
1-888-BIG LAKE (888-244-5253)
Outlet Store: 310 E. Superior St., Duluth, MN 55802